THE MUSIC OF
SIR PETER MAXWELL DAVIES

Sir Peter Maxwell Davies.   Sherwood Fohrmann

THE MUSIC OF
SIR PETER MAXWELL DAVIES

An annotated catalogue

Edited by

Colin Bayliss

WILTSHIRE
COUNTY COUNCIL
LIBRARY &
MUSEUM SERVICE

British Library Cataloguing in Publication Data

The music of Sir Peter Maxwell Davies: an
annotated catalogue.
I. Bayliss, Colin, 1948-
780.942

ISBN 0-948929-46-4

Published by Highgate Publications (Beverley) Ltd.
24 Wylies Road, Beverley, HU17 7AP
Telephone (0482) 866826

Printed by B.A. Press, Unit 7A, Tokenspire Park,
Hull Road, Woodmansey, Beverley, HU17 0TB
Telephone (0482) 882232

*Front cover: Sir Peter Maxwell Davies pictured at his croft on the island of Hoy in the
Orkneys.*

Ros Drinkwater — The Sunday Times

CONTENTS

PHOTOGRAPHS

EDITOR'S PREFACE AND ACKNOWLEDGEMENTS

SIR PETER MAXWELL DAVIES is now recognised as one of Britain's, and indeed one of the world's, leading composers and I consider it an honour to produce a catalogue of his musical works.

For the second time in a year, I find myself in the unusual position of writing a preface to such a catalogue, unusual as a result of the speed at which I was able to move from the cataloguing of Anthony Hedges' works to those of Sir Peter. This speed was only possible with the invaluable help and co-operation that I have received from various sources, which I must now gratefully acknowledge.

The idea for this catalogue arose from discussions with staff at the City of Salford's Cultural Services Department. A large amount of Sir Peter's early manuscripts and sketches had been deposited at the Salford Archive Centre, and it was originally intended to produce a working list of this material internally. My discussions with the Cultural Services Manager, Mr Royston Futter, however, produced the necessary co-operation of Mr Andrew Cross of the Archive Centre, and also Messrs Tim Ashworth and Tony Frankland of the Local History Library at the Salford Art Gallery to incorporate this information into a projected full-scale catalogue. Similar discussions with Miss Ann Mackay of the Scottish Music Information Centre elicited her willing assistance.

Information on recordings has been given by the National Sound Archive in South Kensington, and holders of private manuscript material have been generous in their co-operation. The layout was designed by Andi Chapple, who also type-set the catalogue from my near-illegible original notes, for which I hold his ability in great awe. To all these people I give my thanks.

I must of course thank Sir Peter himself for his blessing on the undertaking and for the time spent on verifying certain details, but above all, the co-operation of one person was vital. This was Sir Peter's manager, Mrs Judy Arnold. She most kindly allowed me the use of all the information which she had amassed over a period of fifteen years about Sir Peter's music and indeed allowed me to quote such information verbatim from her marketing catalogues when I wished to do so, thus saving me many months of research. I was also able to inspect manuscript material in her possession, furnishing valuable information, and she has been enormously helpful in assisting me to trace the owners of privately-held manuscripts. I must also thank her for allowing me to use the photographs, of which she is the copyright-holder. As it will fall upon her to continue the numbering system of the catalogue for future editions, it was suggested by Sir Peter that the catalogue numbers be preceded by the letter J, to which I agreed wholeheartedly. She tells me that she is delighted with the outcome of our co-operation, and I therefore in gratitude dedicate this book to her.

Colin Bayliss
Hedon, East Yorkshire, January 1991

INTRODUCTION

THIS CATALOGUE follows the normal format in that it is numbered in chronological order. Further output by the composer, whether published or unpublished, can therefore be numbered with ease in the future.

The list includes all known published and unpublished works, together with the location of the manuscripts and sketches where these are known.

Most manuscript material until about 1971 has been deposited with Salford City Archives (abbreviated in the catalogue to S.A.C.) at the Archive Centre at 658-662, Liverpool Road, Irlam, Salford M30 5AD (Tel.: 061 775 5643). This represents the composer's recognition of his birth in Salford and childhood at Swinton, now part of the City of Salford administrative area.

Much of the remaining manuscript material from 1971 onwards has been deposited with the Scottish Music Information Centre (abbreviated in the catalogue to S.M.I.C.) at 1, Bowmont Gardens, Glasgow G12 9LB (Tel.: 041 334 6393) to reflect Sir Peter's identification with Scotland since moving to the Orkneys at that time. Other manuscripts are in private hands and have been identified and located where this was possible. It would be greatly appreciated if the holders of missing manuscripts or other unpublished material which has not been traced by the Editor, would contact Sir Peter's manager, Mrs Judy Arnold, at 50, Hogarth Road, London SW5 0PU (Tel.: 071 370 1477).

Recording details include deleted titles. Where record numbers of the same pressing have changed, all numbers have been given where possible. It is possible that private recordings have been made of works not otherwise recorded. If these are not in breach of existing copyright, copies of these recordings would be welcomed by the National Sound Archive at 29 Exhibition Road, South Kensington, London SW7 2AS (Tel.: 071 589 6603) to be used for private study only.

Performing times are obviously not rigid and will vary with different performers.

Notes on each work are related to its known history together with an explanation of its structure where it was considered necessary, and no attempt has been made to describe the music, as this has been done previously in Mrs Arnold's marketing catalogues by Paul Griffiths and Stephen Pruslin. The analysis section has been left unfilled for certain works as the large number of changes of tempo would be meaningless in a catalogue format.

Those who wish to read of Sir Peter's life are recommended to the following publications:

Peter Maxwell Davies: Studies from two decades
Selected and introduced by Stephen Pruslin
TEMPO booklet no. 2, 1979.   104pp.   Includes contributions from Michael Chanan, Jonathan Harvey, Gabriel Josipovici, Oliver Knussen, Anthony Payne and the composer himself.

Peter Maxwell Davies
By Paul Griffiths
London: Robson Books, 1982. 196 pp.

Peter Maxwell Davies: Ein Komponistenporträt
Ed. Renate Jeutner (Musik der Zeit Dokumentationen und Studien Nr. 3)
Bonn: Boosey and Hawkes, 1983. 182 pp.

Please note that all material listed in this catalogue is covered by current copyright and performing rights legislation, and any application to perform, reproduce or purchase any of this material should be addressed to the appropriate publishers or to Sir Peter's manager, Mrs Judy Arnold.

Colin Bayliss

EARLY PIANO PIECE I   (?1942)

Catalogue no.:   J1

Descriptive title: UNTITLED (Early Piano Piece I)

Musical format: Piano solo

Location of manuscript: S.A.C. (MS)

Analysis: *Moderato*

Performance length:

Composed: ?1942   **Revised:**

Instruments: Piano

Publishing information: MS (3 pp)

Recording details:

First performance:

       at:

       by:

Notes: Undated MS in the S.A.C., in an envelope marked 'Piano piece age 8'

INCANTATIONS I and II   (1947)

Catalogue no.:   J2

Descriptive title: INCANTATIONS I and II

Musical format: Piano solo

Location of manuscript: S.A.C. (MS)

Analysis: (i) *Adagio* (ii) *Più mosso - lento, ben marcato*

Performance length:

Composed: 1947   **Revised:**

Instruments: Piano

Publishing information: MS (4 pp)

Recording details:

First performance:

    at:

    by:

Notes: The MS contains pencil notes for possible orchestration
of no. (ii). See also *Prelude* [J6].

BIRDS   (?1948)

Descriptive title: THE BIRDS

Musical format: Voice and piano

Location of manuscript: S.A.C. (MS)

Analysis: *Allegretto*, clearly, cheerfully

Performance length:

Composed: ?1948   **Revised:**

Instruments: Voice (treble clef) and piano

Publishing information: MS (1 p)

Recording details:

First performance:

>   **at:**

>   **by:**

Notes: Words by Moira O'Neill.   Marked as composed 15.1.1948, with a pencil insert of "Long before this date", and an ink note of composition December 1947.

CLOUD   (1948)

Catalogue no.:   J4

Descriptive title: THE CLOUD

Musical format: Piano solo

Location of manuscript: S.A.C. (MS)

Analysis: *Andante tranquillo*

Performance length:

Composed: 1948   **Revised:**

Instruments: Piano

Publishing information: MS (4 pp)

Recording details:

First performance:

      at:

      by:

Notes: Marked "2nd copy". Dated 20 May 1948, with a note
that the first copy was dated 13 February 1948.

RIVER   (1948)

Catalogue no.:   J5

Descriptive title: THE RIVER (part 2)

Musical format: Piano solo

Location of manuscript: S.A.C. (MS)

Analysis: *Moderato - allegro con fuoco*

Performance length:

Composed: 1948   **Revised:**

Instruments: Piano

Publishing information: MS (2 pp)

Recording details:

First performance:

    at:

    by:

Notes: 1 page of MS on the back of the final sheet of *The Cloud* [J4]. The other on the back of a sketch for an adagio and fugue for string quartet, heavily crossed out, and not given an entry in the catalogue.

PRELUDE   (1949)

Catalogue no.:   J6

Descriptive title: PRELUDE (early piano piece)

Musical format: Piano solo

Location of manuscript: S.A.C. (MS)

Analysis: *Lento*

Performance length:

Composed: 1949   **Revised:**

Instruments: Piano

Publishing information: MS (2 pp)

Recording details:

First performance:

      at:

      by:

Notes: The MS contains pencil notes for possible orchestration
and is in a folder with *Incantations I and II* [J2].

FUNERAL MARCH IN B MAJOR

(later 1940s)

Catalogue no.: J7

Descriptive title: FUNERAL MARCH IN B MAJOR (for a pig)

Musical format: Piano solo

Location of manuscript: Unkown

Analysis:

Performance length:

Composed: later 1940s **Revised:**

Instruments: Piano

Publishing information: MS

Recording details:

First performance:

 at:

 by:

Notes: For Mr Major, then headmaster of Leigh Grammar School. This is all that the composer can remember of this piece, which the Editor has been unable to trace. If it should be re-discovered, please contact Mrs Judy Arnold.

RILKE SETTING   (?1950)

Catalogue no.:   J8

Descriptive title: UNTITLED (Rilke Setting)

Musical format: Unaccompanied chorus

Location of manuscript: S.A.C. (MS)

Analysis:

Performance length:

Composed: ?1950   **Revised:**

Instruments: Treble, Alto, Tenor, Bass

Publishing information: MS (2 pp)

Recording details:

First performance:

      at:

      by:

Notes: A setting of Rainer Maria Rilke's *Tenth Duino Elegy*,
'Stehn am Fuss des Gebirgs'. Date and signature have
been erased but the date may be interpreted as 1950.

FIVE SONGS TO POEMS BY MORGENSTERN (?1950)

Catalogue no.:   **J9**

Descriptive title: FIVE SONGS TO POEMS BY MORGENSTERN

Musical format: Voice(s) and instruments

Location of manuscript: S.A.C. (MS)

Analysis: (i) Leise Lieder (ii) Parabol (iii) Oh, wie so lieb, als ich, mein zartes Vöglein (iv) Ein Schmetterling (v) Sehnsucht

Performance length:

Composed: ?1950   **Revised:**

Instruments: Soprano, flute, clarinet, harp and string quartet

Publishing information: MS (20 pp)

Recording details:

First performance:

      at:

      by:

Notes: MS undated and written under a pseudonym now totally erased.

EARLY PIANO PIECE II   (?1952)

Catalogue no.:   J10

Descriptive title: UNTITLED (Early Piano Piece II)

Musical format: Piano solo

Location of manuscript: S.A.C. (MS)

Analysis: *Andante*

Performance length:

Composed: ?1952   **Revised:**

Instruments: Piano

Publishing information: MS (4 pp)

Recording details:

First performance:

     at:

     by:

Notes: Undated, but placed in an envelope in S.A.C. with other material and tentatively dated at 1952 by the style of the hand.

PIANO DUET   (1952)

Catalogue no.:   J11

Descriptive title: UNTITLED (Piano duet)

Musical format: Piano duet

Location of manuscript: S.A.C. (MS)

Analysis: *Allegretto, con moto*

Performance length:

Composed: 1952   **Revised:**

Instruments: Two pianos

Publishing information: MS (7 pp)

Recording details:

First performance:

      at:

      by:

Notes:

QUARTET MOVEMENT (1952)

Catalogue no.:   J12

Descriptive title:	QUARTET MOVEMENT
Musical format:	String quartet
Location of manuscript:	S.A.C. (MS and sketch)

Analysis: *Allegro vivace*

Performance length: 5 minutes

Composed: 1952   **Revised:**

Instruments: String quartet

Publishing information: CHESTER MUSIC. Miniature score for sale (19 pp); parts on sale separately

Recording details:

First performance: May 23 1983

    at: Barbican House, London, at the 40th Anniversary Gala of the Society for the Promotion of New Music

    by: The Arditti String Quartet

Notes: A tape recording is available in the National Sound Archive for private study only.

PIANO SONATA (unpublished)   (1954)

Catalogue no.:   J13

Descriptive title: PIANO SONATA (unpublished)

Musical format: Piano solo

Location of manuscript: Ian Kellam

Analysis: (i) *Lento - moderato* (ii) *Vivace ma non troppo allegro* (iii) *Adagio, alla marcia - Lento* (iv) *Allegro moderato con vivo (il tempo sempre in relievo nella fuga) - Vivace con strepito*

Performance length: 28 minutes

Composed: 1954   **Revised:**

Instruments: Piano

Publishing information: MS (32 pp)

Recording details:

First performance:

       at:

       by:

Notes: Written for Ian Kellam on his 21st birthday, May 17 1954.

WOODWIND OCTET (1954)

Catalogue no.:　　J14

Descriptive title:　　　　WOODWIND OCTET

Musical format:　　　　Octet

Location of manuscript:　　S.A.C. (MS)

Analysis:　　(i) Overture: *Moderato con moto* (ii) Alla austriaca: *Ländlertempo* (iii) Intermezzo: *Adagio* (iv) Americanismo: *Allegretto con moto*

Performance length:

Composed:　1954　　　　**Revised:**

Instruments:　Piccolo, flute, oboe, cor anglais, clarinet, bass clarinet, two bassoons

Publishing information:　　MS (10 pp)

Recording details:

First performance:

　　　　at:

　　　　by:

Notes:

ILLA AUTEM ARBOR (?1955)

Catalogue no.:   J15

Descriptive title: ILLA AUTEM ARBOR: Motet

Musical format: Unaccompanied chorus

Location of manuscript: S.A.C. (Sketch)

Analysis:

Performance length:

Composed: ?1955   **Revised:**

Instruments: Soprano, Soprano, Alto, Alto

Publishing information: MS (1 p)

Recording details:

First performance:

       at:

       by:

Notes: Sketch only. Marked 'unpublished'.

UNFINISHED SKETCHES I   (mid 1950s)

Catalogue no.:   J16

Descriptive title: UNTITLED (Unfinished Sketches I)

Musical format:

Location of manuscript: S.A.C. (Sketch)

Analysis:

Performance length:

Composed: mid 1950s   **Revised:**

Instruments:

Publishing information: MS (i) 75 pp (ii) 74 pp (iii) 2 pp

Recording details:

First performance:

      at:

      by:

Notes: In a folder marked "Orchestral work of mid 1950s". (i) Mainly of orchestral work(s) though with some piano (?) music and a scheme for a set of variations on a theme of Tomkins. (ii) In a folder marked "Manchester General": Including exercises, sketches for *Te Lucis Ante Terminum* and ragas. (iii) In a folder marked "i. Counterpoint exercise ii. Analysis".

BURCHIELLO (1955)

Catalogue no.: J17

Descriptive title:	BURCHIELLO for Instruments of Percussion
Musical format:	Sixteen percussionists - eleven unpitched, five pitched
Location of manuscript:	Ian Kellam

Analysis: (i) *Allegro non troppo* (ii) *Lento molto* (iii) *Molto presto*

Performance length: 16 minutes

Composed: 1955 **Revised:**

Instruments: Small suspended cymbal (doubling large suspended cymbal, triangle and side drum with snares), tenor drum (doubling small gong and tam-tam), cymbals, two bass drums (one muted), three temple blocks, wood block (doubling side drum without snares and cymbal in third movement), castanets, tambourine, maracas, glockenspiel, xylophone, vibraphone, tubular bells (D, E, G flat, G natural, A, B flat, C, D, F natural, G natural in ascending order)

Publishing information: MS (51 pp)

Recording details:

First performance:

at:

by:

Notes:

TRUMPET SONATA   (1955)

Catalogue no.:   J18

Descriptive title: SONATA FOR TRUMPET AND PIANO
(Op. 1)

Musical format: Trumpet and piano

Location of manuscript: S.A.C. (MS and sketches)

Analysis: (i) *Allegro moderato* (ii) *Lento* (iii) *Allegro vivo*

Performance length: 7 minutes

Composed: 1955   **Revised:**

Instruments: Trumpet in D, piano

Publishing information: SCHOTT. Performing score with
trumpet part for sale. (Score 16 pp)

Recording details: NONESUCH: Record, H71275. Gerard
Schwarz, trumpet; Ursula Oppens,
piano.
BIS: CD, 287.   Håken Hardenberger,
trumpet; Roland Pöntinen, piano.
CRYSTAL: CD, 665. Thomas Stevens,
trumpet; Zia Carno, piano.

First performance: 1955

at: Manchester University, Arthur Worthington Hall

by: Elgar Howarth, trumpet and John Ogden, piano

Notes: The fanfare motif in the first movement also opens the
opera *Taverner*. Tape recordings of other performances
by R. Anderson, trumpet and S. Bradshaw, piano, and
also by Elgar Howarth, trumpet and J. Constable, piano
are available at the National Sound Archive for private
study only.

FIVE PIECES FOR PIANO   (1956)

Catalogue no.:   J19

Descriptive title: FIVE PIECES FOR PIANO (Op. 2)

Musical format: Piano solo

Location of manuscript: S.A.C. (MS and sketches)

Analysis: (i) *Andante* (ii) *Allegro* (iii) *Andante* (iv) *Adagio* (v) *Allegretto*

Performance length: 15 minutes

Composed: 1956   **Revised:**

Instruments: Piano

Publishing information: SCHOTT. Score (24 pp) for sale.

Recording details: HMV: Record, ALP 2029. John Ogden, piano
                                HMV: Record, ASD 645. John Ogden, piano.

First performance: December 1956

    at: Liverpool

    by: John Ogden, piano

Notes: A tape recording of the pieces performed by David Wilde is available at the National Sound Archive for private study only.

STEDMAN DOUBLES   (1956)

Catalogue no.:   J20

Descriptive title: STEDMAN DOUBLES for Clarinet and Percussion

Musical format: Clarinet and percussion

Location of manuscript: S.A.C. (MS and sketches)

Analysis: See Notes

Performance length: Up to 30 minutes (variable)

Composed: 1956   **Revised:**   1968

Instruments: Clarinet

Percussion (one player): Pair of bongos, 2 tabla (large and small), mridangam, 3 suspended cymbals, wood block, side drum, tenor drum, bass drum, tam-tam, 4 small finger drums, pair of antique or finger cymbals

Publishing information: BOOSEY AND HAWKES. Score (18 pp) for sale.

Recording details:

First performance: April 23 1968

at: Cardiff University

by: Alan Hacker, clarinet and Tristan Fry, percussion

continued ...

Notes: Written for Alan Hacker and Tristan Fry. The idea of having a soloist accompanied and stimulated by unpitched percussion came from Indian music, but Davies's raga is in the form of a three-part Christian hymn, and its processes, as the title suggests, relate to change ringing. There is also a sonata hidden in the structure, comprising a first movement with slow introduction (and improvised cadenzas), an adagio and a presto finale.

The original version was never performed, and had three players (two percussionists and clarinet).

A tape recording with Alan Hacker, clarinet and B. Quinn, percussion is available at the National Sound Archive for private study only.

The Fires of London with Sir Peter Maxwell Davies at the 1983 Bath Festival.

Martin Haswell

CLARINET SONATA (1956)

Catalogue no.:   J21

Descriptive title: SONATA FOR CLARINET AND PIANO

Musical format: Clarinet and piano

Location of manuscript: S.A.C. (sketches)

Analysis: (i) *Moderato* (ii) *Allegro* (iii)*Adagio*

Performance length: 25 minutes

Composed: 1956   **Revised:**

Instruments: Clarinet and piano

Publishing information: CHESTER MUSIC. Performing score
with clarinet part for sale and for hire
(Score 32 pp).

Recording details:

First performance: July 20 1957

    at: Darmstadt Festival

    by: Georgina Dobrée, clarinet and the composer, piano

Notes: Written for Harrison Birtwistle.

ALMA REDEMPTORIS MATER   (1957)

Catalogue no.:   J22

Descriptive title: ALMA REDEMPTORIS MATER

Musical format: Wind sextet

Location of manuscript: S.A.C. (sketch)

Analysis: (i) *Andante* (ii) *Presto* (iii) *Andante* (without a break)

Performance length: 6 minutes

Composed: 1957   **Revised:**

Instruments: Flute, oboe, two clarinets, bassoon, horn

Publishing information: SCHOTT. Miniature score (12 pp) for sale; miniature score and parts for hire.

Recording details:

First performance: May 7 1957

    at: Dartington Summer School

    by: The New Music Ensemble, conducted by John Carewe

Notes: The title refers to the plainsong melody and also the motet of John Dunstable used in this piece and based on the same melody. A tape recording of the Pierrot Players, conducted by the composer, is available at the National Sound Archive for private study only.

SAINT MICHAEL SONATA   (1957)

Catalogue no.:   J23

Descriptive title: SAINT MICHAEL SONATA for 17 Wind
                                  Instruments

Musical format: Wind ensemble

Location of manuscript: S.A.C. (MS)

Analysis: (i) *Moderato* (ii) *Allegro* (iii) *Lento molto* (iv) *Allegro*
                      (v) *Adagio*

Performance length: 17 minutes

Composed: 1957   **Revised:**

Instruments: Two flutes, two oboes, two clarinets in B flat, two
                    bassoons, three horns, trumpet in D, trumpet in B flat,
                    two trombones, bass trombone and tuba

Publishing information: SCHOTT. Miniature score (64 pp) for
                                  sale and hire; parts for hire.

Recording details: LOUISVILLE ORCHESTRA RECORDS:
                                  Record, L 5756.   Members of the
                                  Louisville Orchestra conducted by
                                  Jorge Mester.

First performance: 13 July 1959

        at: Cheltenham Town Hall

        by: Members of the London Symphony Orchestra
                  conducted by the composer

Notes: In the dramatic manner of Giovanni Gabrieli with
                    separate choirs of woodwind and brass. A tape
                    recording by the BBC Northern Orchestra, conducted
                    by Meredith Davies, is available at the National Sound
                    Archive, as are records of performances by the
                    London Sinfonietta, conducted by Elgar Howarth,
                    and also of the first performance. These are for
                    private study only.

SEXTET   (1958)

Catalogue no.:   **J24**

Descriptive title: SEXTET

Musical format: Sextet

Location of manuscript: S.A.C. (MS and sketches)

Analysis: *Adagio - allegro vivace - andante - allegro - quasi recitativo - allegro vivace*

Performance length:

Composed: 1958   **Revised:**   1971

Instruments: Flute, clarinet in A, bass clarinet, violin, cello and piano

Publishing information: MS (16 pp)

Recording details:

First performance: 1958

>   **at:**   Dartington Summer School

>   **by:**   The New Music Ensemble, conducted by John Carewe

Notes: 'Withdrawn' by the composer. The piece was intended to be re-written into a septet. A cello part for this is in the collection at S.M.I.C. and two other parts with "sextet" amended to "septet" are at present with Mrs Judy Arnold. The piano part was removed and a guitar part substituted. The work was never published in either form, although the septet parts are marked as received by Schott.

PROLATION FOR ORCHESTRA   (1958)

Catalogue no.:   J25

Descriptive title: PROLATION FOR ORCHESTRA

Musical format: Full orchestra

Location of manuscript: S.A.C. (MS and sketches)

Analysis: One continuous movement

Performance length: 20 minutes

Composed: 1958   **Revised:**

Instruments: Piccolo, two flutes, two oboes, cor anglais, three clarinets, two bassoons (second doubling contrabassoon), four horns, three trumpets, four trombones, tuba, timpani

Percussion (3 players): bass drum, bass drum (muffled), glockenspiel, five suspended cymbals, xylophone

Publishing information: SCHOTT. Miniature score (98 pp) for sale; full score and parts for hire

Recording details:

First performance: July 1959

          at: Rome (I.S.C.M. Festival)

          by: Orchestra of Radio-Televisione Italiana conducted by Nino Sanzogno

Notes: Awarded the Olivetti Prize in 1959. Prolation governed the relative proportion of minim and semibreve in the mediaeval rhythmic modal system. A tape recording of a performance by the New Philharmonia Orchestra, conducted by Norman Del Mar, is available at the National Sound Archive for private study only.

CAROL FOR JULIAN BREAM　　　(1958)

Catalogue no.:　　J26

Descriptive title:　　　　CAROL FOR JULIAN BREAM

Musical format:　　　　Voice and guitar

Location of manuscript:　　S.A.C. (MS)

Analysis:　　Voice and guitar

Performance length:

Composed:　　1958　　　　**Revised:**

Instruments:　　Voice and guitar

Publishing information:　　MS (1 p)

Recording details:

First performance:

　　　　at:

　　　　by:

Notes:　　　　The seven bars of music end with the direction to gain the desired effects by "the guitar being brought to bear sharply upon the head of the singer, whose note thus effects a harmonious union and identity with the tones of the instrument, upon his head appearing through it".

DANTE SETTINGS   (late 1950s)

Catalogue no.:   J27

Descriptive title: DANTE SETTINGS (unfinished)

Musical format: Voice(s) and instruments

Location of manuscript: S.A.C. (sketches)

Analysis:

Performance length:

Composed: late 1950s   **Revised:**

Instruments: Voice in bass clef and orchestra (see notes)

Publishing information: MS (14 pp)

Recording details:

First performance:

at:

by:

Notes: Sketches show some indication of instrumentation, e.g. Flute, oboe, clarinet, bass clarinet, horn, trombone, tuba, bassoon, contrabassoon, glockenspiel, timpani, two harps and strings.

RICERCAR AND DOUBLES (1959)

Catalogue no.:   J28

Descriptive title: RICERCAR AND DOUBLES on 'To Many a Well' for Ensemble

Musical format: Octet

Location of manuscript: S.A.C. (MS and sketches)

Analysis: Ricercar - *Andante non troppo*; Double I - *Allegro molto*; Double II - *Lento*

Performance length: 12 minutes

Composed: 1959   **Revised:**

Instruments: Flute, oboe, clarinet in B flat, bassoon, horn, harpsichord, viola and cello

Publishing information: SCHOTT. Miniature score (20 pp) for sale and hire; parts for hire.

Recording details:

First performance: 1959

      at: Dartmouth Festival, New Hampshire, USA

      by:

Notes: Commissioned by the Dartmouth Festival. Based on a mediaeval English carol (in *Musica Britannia* Vol. IV no. 114). A tape recording of a performance by the Virtuoso Ensemble, conducted by John Carewe, is available at the National Sound Archive for private study only.

FIVE MOTETS   (1959)

Catalogue no.:   J29

Descriptive title: FIVE MOTETS

Musical format: Chorus and instruments

Location of manuscript: S.A.C. (MS)

Analysis: (i) *Spes, via, vita* (ii) *Alma redemptoris mater* (iii) *O lux quam non videt alia lux* (iv) *Nec mora, carnifice gemini* (v) *Attolite portes principes*

Performance length: 18 minutes

Composed: 1959   **Revised:**

Instruments: *Centre*: Soli, violins 1 and 2, viola, cello, double bass.
Left: Choir I (SATB), two trumpets, two trombones, chamber organ I.
Right: Choir II (SATB), flute, oboe, clarinet, bassoon, contrabassoon, chamber organ II.

Publishing information: BOOSEY AND HAWKES. Study score (47 pp) and vocal score (72 pp) for sale and hire; instrumental parts for hire.

Recording details:

First performance: March 1 1965

    at: A MacNaughton Concert at the St. Pancras Festival at Friends House, Euston Road

    by: The Ambrosian Singers and The English Chamber Orchestra, conducted by Norman Del Mar.

continued ...

Notes: Davies' first published vocal work, described as a personal reaction to what was newest in Stravinsky's output. Originally written for voice alone, the instruments are used mostly to double the voices.

The groups should be spaced as far apart as is practical to achieve a real antiphony. If necessary, each group may have its own conductor.

A tape recording of the first performance is available at the National Sound Archive for private study only.

Sir Peter Maxwell Davies with Orkney Children.   The Sunday Times

FIVE KLEE PICTURES (1959)

Catalogue no.:   J30

Descriptive title: FIVE KLEE PICTURES for school orchestra

Musical format: Junior orchestra

Location of manuscript: Mrs Judy Arnold (Sketches)

Analysis: (i) A Crusader (ii) Oriental garden (iii) The twittering machine (iv) Stained glass saint (v) Ad Parnassum

Performance length: 10 minutes

Composed: 1959   **Revised:**   1976

Instruments: Two flutes, two oboes, two bassoons, four horns, two trumpets, piano, strings
Percussion (5 players): side drum, bass drum, cymbals, castanets, wood block, 4 temple blocks, tam-tam, tambourine, triangle, nightingale and xylophone

Publishing information: BOOSEY AND HAWKES. Full score (24 pp) and set of parts for sale and hire.

Recording details:

First performance: (Final version) October 16 1976

    at: St. John's Smith Square, London

    by: Young Musicians' Symphony Orchestra, conducted by James Blair.

continued ...

Notes: The original version was composed for Cirencester Grammar School and was performed at the school by the School Orchestra, conducted by the composer, in 1959. The work was inspired by paintings by Paul Klee. The sketches are in a bag marked "Cirencester Sketches". The original version was lost, and the revised version was re-written from the surviving parts. A tape recording of a performance by the BBC Symphony Orchestra, conducted by Gennady Rozhdestvensky, is available at the National Sound Archive for private study only.

WILLIAM BYRD: THREE DANCES (1959)

Catalogue no.:   J31

Descriptive title: WILLIAM BYRD: THREE DANCES
arranged for school orchestra

Musical format: Junior orchestra

Location of manuscript: Mrs Judy Arnold (Sketches)

Analysis: (i) La Volta (ii) Alman (iii) Coranto

Performance length: 4 minutes

Composed: 1959   **Revised:**

Instruments: Two flutes, two oboes, two clarinets, bassoon, horn,
two trumpets, trombone, guitar, strings
Percussion (1 player): tambourine and tabor

Publishing information: SCHOTT. Score (11 pp) and parts for
sale.

Recording details:

First performance: 1959

at: Cirencester Grammar School

by: Cirencester School Orchestra, conducted by the
composer

Notes: The sketches are in a bag marked "Cirencester
Sketches".

FOUR CANONS   (1959)

Catalogue no.:   J32

Descriptive title: Four canons

Musical format: Junior orchestra

Location of manuscript: Mrs Judy Arnold (Sketches and incomplete MS)

Analysis: (i) Direct canon (ii) Direct and inverse canon (iii) Canon on a theme of chords with melismatic improvisation

Performance length:

Composed: 1959   **Revised:**

Instruments: Orchestra of Violin I, violin II, cello, piano

Publishing information: MS

Recording details:

First performance: February 3 1960

at: School Library, Cirencester Grammar School

by: Cirencester Grammar School Junior Orchestra

Notes: In a bag of manuscripts marked 'Cirencester Sketches'.

PAVAN AND GALLIARD   (1959)

Catalogue no.:   J33

Descriptive title: PAVAN AND GALLIARD

Musical format: Junior orchestra

Location of manuscript: Mrs Judy Arnold (Sketches and incomplete MS)

Analysis: (i) *Grave* (ii) *Allegro moderato*

Performance length:

Composed: 1959   **Revised:**

Instruments: Orchestra of Violin I, violin II, cello, piano

Publishing information: MS

Recording details:

First performance: February 3 1960

     at: School Library, Cirencester Grammar School

     by: Cirencester Grammar School Junior Orchestra

Notes: In a bag of manuscripts marked 'Cirencester Sketches'.

SATIE: PRELUDE FROM
JACK-IN-THE-BOX   (?1960)

Catalogue no.:   J34

Descriptive title: PRELUDE from *Jack-in-the-Box*: Satie,
                            arranged Maxwell Davies

Musical format: Junior orchestra

Location of manuscript: Mrs Judy Arnold (Sketches)

Analysis:

Performance length:

Composed: ?1960   Revised:

Instruments:

Publishing information: MS

Recording details:

First performance:

      at:

      by:

Notes: Arranged for Cirencester Grammar School Orchestra,
            and presumably performed there. In a bag of
            manuscripts marked 'Cirencester Sketches'.

MILHAUD: ROMANCE FROM
TROIS RAG-CAPRICES   (?1960)

Catalogue no.:   J35

Descriptive title: ROMANCE from *Trois Rag-Caprices*:
Milhaud, arranged Maxwell Davies

Musical format: Junior orchestra

Location of manuscript: Mrs Judy Arnold (Sketches)

Analysis:

Performance length:

Composed: ?1960   **Revised:**

Instruments:

Publishing information: MS

Recording details:

First performance:

    at:

    by:

Notes: Arranged for Cirencester Grammar School Orchestra, and presumably performed there. In a bag of manuscripts marked 'Cirencester Sketches'.

POULENC: MOUVEMENT PERPETUEL no.1 (?1960)

Catalogue no.:   J36

Descriptive title: MOUVEMENT PERPETUEL no.1:
                              Poulenc, arranged Maxwell Davies

Musical format: Junior orchestra

Location of manuscript: Mrs Judy Arnold (Sketches)

Analysis:

Performance length:

Composed: ?1960   **Revised:**

Instruments:

Publishing information: MS

Recording details:

First performance:

     at:

     by:

Notes: Arranged for Cirencester Grammar School Orchestra, and presumably performed there. In a bag of manuscripts marked 'Cirencester Sketches'.

WATKINS ALE   (?1960)

Catalogue no.:   J37

Descriptive title: WATKINS ALE: Anon., arranged
                                Maxwell Davies

Musical format: Junior orchestra

Location of manuscript: Mrs Judy Arnold

Analysis:

Performance length:

Composed: ?1960   **Revised:**

Instruments: Violin I, violin II, cello, flute, oboe, clarinet, horn,
                    xylophone, piano

Publishing information: MS (1 p)

Recording details:

First performance:

      at:

      by:

Notes: Undated manuscript in a bag of manuscripts marked
                  'Cirencester Studies'.

BENEDICAM DOMINO (1960)

Catalogue no.:   J38

Descriptive title: BENEDICAM DOMINO: Johnson (from the *Mulliner Book*), arranged Maxwell Davies

Musical format: Wind ensemble

Location of manuscript: Mrs Judy Arnold (Sketch)

Analysis: (i) *Adagio* (ii) *Moderato* (iii) *Allegro*

Performance length:

Composed: 1960   **Revised:**

Instruments: Two flutes, two oboes, two clarinets, bassoon, two trumpets, horn

Publishing information: MS

Recording details:

First performance:

    at:

    by:

Notes: The sketches are marked 'For the wind section of the orchestra, Cirencester Grammar School, May 1960'. In a bag of manuscripts marked 'Cirencester Sketches'.

O MAGNUM MYSTERIUM (1960)

Catalogue no.:   J39

Descriptive title:	O MAGNUM MYSTERIUM
Musical format:	Unaccompanied chorus
Location of manuscript:	S.A.C. (MS and sketches)

Analysis: (i) *O Magnum Mysterium* (S, SA, SATB) (ii) Haylle, comly and clene (SATB) (iii) *Alleluia, pro Virgine Maria* (SATB) (iv) The fader of Heaven (SA)

Performance length: 40 minutes (12 minutes SATB)

Composed: 1960   **Revised:**

Instruments: Soprano, Alto, Tenor and Bass chorus, Ensemble (14 players), organ

Publishing information: SCHOTT. Score (20 pp) and parts for sale.

Recording details: ARGO: Record, ZRG 5327; Record (mono), RG 327; Record, 5-BBA 1015. Cirencester Grammar School Choir and Orchestra with Simon Preston, organ, conducted by the composer.
COLLINS CLASSICS: CD, 12702; Cassette, 12704. The Sixteen, conducted by Harry Christopher.

First performance: December 8 1960

   at: Cirencester Parish Church

   by: Choir of Cirencester Grammar School, conducted by the composer.

Notes: Each carol may be performed separately or in combination with any of the others. See also *Organ Fantasia on 'O Magnum Mysterium'* [J40]. The above recordings are also available for private study at the National Sound Archive.

ORGAN FANTASIA ON 'O MAGNUM MYSTERIUM' (1960)

Catalogue no.: J40

Descriptive title: ORGAN FANTASIA on 'O Magnum Mysterium'

Musical format: Organ solo

Location of manuscript: S.A.C. (MS and sketches)

Analysis: Organ solo

Performance length: 15 minutes

Composed: 1960   **Revised:**

Instruments: Organ

Publishing information: SCHOTT. Score (7 pp) for sale.

Recording details: ARGO: Record, ZRG 5327; Record (mono), RG 327. Simon Preston, organ.

First performance: December 8 1960

    at: Cirencester Parish Church

    by: Alan Wicks, organ

Notes: The organ fantasia may be performed separately or in combination with the carols and/or sonatas (see [J39])..

FIVE VOLUNTARIES   (1960)

Catalogue no.:   J41

Descriptive title: FIVE VOLUNTARIES arranged for
school orchestra

Musical format: Junior orchestra

Location of manuscript: Mrs Judy Arnold (Sketches)

Analysis: (i) March Time (William Croft) (ii) Serenade (Jeremiah
Clarke) (iii) Magnificat (Pierre Attaignant) (iv) Sarabande
(Louis Couperin) (v) King William's March (Jeremiah
Clarke)

Performance length: 10 minutes

Composed: 1960   **Revised:**

Instruments: Three flutes, three oboes, two clarinets, bassoon, two
horns, three trumpets (in B flat or C), two trombones,
continuo, strings
Percussion (1 player): cymbal, side drum, bass drum

Publishing information: SCHOTT. Score (15 pp) and parts for
sale.

Recording details:

First performance: 1960

    at: Cirencester Grammar School

    by: Cirencester Grammar School Orchestra, conducted
by the composer

Notes: The sketches are in a bag marked "Cirencester
Sketches".

MONTEVERDI: IL BALLO DELLA INGRATE   (?1961)

Catalogue no.:   J42

Descriptive title: IL BALLO DELLA INGRATE (EXCERPT):
                                Monteverdi, arranged Maxwell Davies for
                                school orchestra

Musical format: Junior orchestra

Location of manuscript: Mrs Judy Arnold (MS)

Analysis: *Allegro moderato - allegro - allegro moderato, adagio -
                  moderato alla marcia*

Performance length:

Composed: ?1961   **Revised:**

Instruments: Three flutes, two oboes, two clarinets, bassoon, horn,
                     trumpet, trombone, strings, piano
                     Percussion: side drum and xylophone

Publishing information: MS

Recording details:

First performance:

      at:

      by:

Notes: For Cirencester Grammar School. In a bag marked
               "Cirencester Sketches".

MONTEVERDI: L'INCORONAZIONE DI POPPEA. RITORNELLO (?1961)

Catalogue no.:   J43

Descriptive title: L'INCORONAZIONE DI POPPEA: RITORNELLO: Monteverdi, arranged Maxwell Davies for school orchestra

Musical format: Junior orchestra

Location of manuscript: Mrs Judy Arnold (MS)

Analysis: *Allegro moderato*

Performance length:

Composed: ?1961   **Revised:**

Instruments: Two flutes, two oboes, three clarinets, bassoon, horn, three trumpets, two trombones, strings, continuo

Publishing information: MS

Recording details:

First performance:

    at:

    by:

Notes: For Cirencester Grammar School. In a bag marked "Cirencester Sketches".

STRING QUARTET   (1961)

Catalogue no.:   J44

Descriptive title: STRING QUARTET

Musical format: String Quartet

Location of manuscript: S.A.C. (Sketch)

Analysis: One continuous movement: *Adagio - allegro - allegro*
                       moderato

Performance length: 13 minutes

Composed: 1961   **Revised:**

Instruments: String quartet

Publishing information: SCHOTT.   Score (20 pp) and parts for
                                     sale.

Recording details:

First performance: November 1961

at: BBC Invitation Concert, Maida Vale Studio

by: The Amici String Quartet

Notes: Written for Alexander Goehr. A record of a performance
                    by the Amici String Quartet, and also a record and a tape
                    recording of a performance by the English String Quartet,
                    are available at the National Sound Archive for private
                    study only.

AVE MARIA, HAIL BLESSED FLOWER (1961)

Catalogue no.:   J45

Descriptive title:	AVE MARIA, HAIL BLESSED FLOWER, carol for SATB chorus
Musical format:	Unaccompanied chorus
Location of manuscript:	Unknown; see notes
Analysis:	
Performance length:	2 minutes
Composed: 1961	**Revised:**
Instruments: Soprano, Alto, Tenor and Bass	
Publishing information:	NOVELLO. Score (4 pp) for sale.
Recording details:	ARGO: Record, ZRG 5446; Record (mono), RG 446. Elizabethan Singers, conducted by Louis Halsey. HMV: Record (mono), CLP 3588; Record, CSD 3588; Record, HQS 1350. Chichester Cathedral Choir, conducted by Birch.
First performance:	1961
at:	Cirencester Grammar School
by:	Choir of Cirencester Grammar School, conducted by the composer
Notes:	The original manuscript was sent to the *Musical Times* but its whereabouts are now unknown, although it was thought to have been through Novello's hands at one time. If this manuscript is rediscovered, please inform Mrs Judy Arnold. The above recordings are available for private study at the National Sound Archive.

TE LUCIS ANTE TERMINUM (1961)

Catalogue no.: J46

Descriptive title: TE LUCIS ANTE TERMINUM for SATB chorus and ensemble

Musical format: Voice(s) and instruments

Location of manuscript: S.A.C. (MS and sketches)

Analysis: Three verses. Instrumental verse (i) *Andante*; Instrumental verse (ii) *Adagio - presto - lento - andante - lento*

Performance length: 11 minutes

Composed: 1961 **Revised:**

Instruments: Soprano, Alto, Tenor and Bass chorus, two flutes, oboe, two clarinets in B flat, two trumpets, two trombones, guitar, cello, glockenspiel

Publishing information: SCHOTT. Miniature, full and choral scores for sale and hire; instrumental parts for hire. Full score 8 pp.

Recording details:

First performance: November 30 1961

at: Cirencester Grammar School

by: Orchestra and Choir of Cirencester Grammar School, conducted by the composer

Notes: Written for the composer's school pupils. The three verses are sung by unaccompanied voices separated by instrumental verses.

RICHARD II　　　　　　　　　　　(1961)

Catalogue no.:　　J47

Descriptive title:　　　　RICHARD II: INCIDENTAL MUSIC

Musical format:

Location of manuscript:　　S.A.C. (Sketches)

Analysis:

Performance length:

Composed:　　1961　　　　**Revised:**

Instruments:

Publishing information:　　MS (11 pp)

Recording details:

First performance:　　　　1962

　　　　at:　　The Old Vic

　　　　by:

Notes:　　　　The manuscript is apparently lost. If it is rediscovered, please contact Mrs Judy Arnold.

NATIONAL ANTHEM   (1961)

Catalogue no.:   J48

Descriptive title: THE NATIONAL ANTHEM.   Arranged
                                Maxwell Davies

Musical format: Junior orchestra

Location of manuscript: Mrs Judy Arnold (Sketch)

Analysis:

Performance length:

Composed: 1961   **Revised:**

Instruments: Flute, oboe, clarinet, trumpet, trombone,
                   glockenspiel, cymbal, tambourine, strings

Publishing information: MS (1 p)

Recording details:

First performance:

    at: Cirencester Grammar School

    by:

Notes: In a bag of manuscripts marked "Cirencester Sketches".

PETER PAN   (1961)

Catalogue no.:   J49

Descriptive title: PETER PAN: INCIDENTAL MUSIC

Musical format: Junior orchestra

Location of manuscript: Mrs Judy Arnold (Sketches and incomplete MS)

Analysis: (i) Overture (ii) Crocodile (iii) Flying (iv) Pillow Fight (v) House Building (vi) Red Indians (vii) Pirates Fighting (viii) Pirates Drunk (ix) Wolves (x) Peter's Kite (xi) Peter's Panpipes (xii) Queen

Performance length:

Composed: 1961   **Revised:**

Instruments: al, tambourine, temple blocks, wood block, viola, cello, double bass

Publishing information: MS

Recording details:

First performance:

      at:

      by:

Notes: In a bag of manuscripts marked "Cirencester Sketches".

MONTEVERDI: VESPERS (1962)

Catalogue no.:   J50

Descriptive title: VESPERS: Monteverdi, arranged for school orchestra Maxwell Davies

Musical format: Junior orchestra and SATB choir

Location of manuscript: Mrs Judy Arnold (MS and sketches)

Analysis:

Performance length:

Composed: 1962   **Revised:**

Instruments: Soprano, Alto, Tenor and Bass chorus, two flutes, two oboes, three clarinets, bassoon, two trumpets, organ, harpsichord and strings (including viola da gamba)

Publishing information: MS

Recording details:

First performance:

      at: Cirencester Grammar School

      by:

Notes: In a bag of manuscripts marked "Cirencester Sketches".

FANTASIA ON AN 'IN NOMINE'
OF JOHN TAVERNER (1962)

Catalogue no.:   J51

Descriptive title:	[FIRST] FANTASIA ON AN 'IN NOMINE' OF JOHN TAVERNER
Musical format:	Full orchestra
Location of manuscript:	Mrs Judy Arnold

Analysis: One continuous movement

Performance length: 11 minutes

Composed: 1962   **Revised:**

Instruments: Two flutes, two oboes, two clarinets, two bassoons, two horns, two trumpets, two trombones, tuba, handbells, crotales (one octave, D flat to D flat in D flat major), strings

Publishing information: SCHOTT. Miniature score (38 pp) for sale; full score and parts for hire.

Recording details:

First performance: September 13 1962

at: Royal Albert Hall, London (BBC Promenade Concert)

by: BBC Symphony Orchestra, conducted by the composer

Notes: Commissioned by the BBC for the Promenade Concerts. A tape recording is available for private study only at the National Sound Archive. See also the *Second Fantasia on an 'In Nomine' of John Taverner* [J57].

page 54

FOUR CAROLS   (1962)

Catalogue no.:   J52

Descriptive title: FOUR CAROLS for SATB chorus

Musical format: Unaccompanied chorus

Location of manuscript: S.A.C. (MS)

Analysis: (i) *Jesus autem hodie* (SATB) (for J.V.B.) (ii) Nowell (SATB) (iii) *Alma redemptoris mater* (4 equal voices) (for P.O.J.) (iv) Carol on St. Steven (SATB)

Performance length: 8 minutes

Composed: 1962   **Revised:**

Instruments: Soprano, Alto, Tenor and Bass

Publishing information: SCHOTT.   Scores of carols for sale separately (25 pp in toto).

Recording details: *Nowell*: DEUTSCHE GRAMMOPHON: CD, 410 590-2GH; Cassette, 410 590-1GH; Record, 410 590-4GH. Westminster Abbey Choir, conducted by Simon Preston.

First performance: 1963

     at: St. Pancras Town Hall, London

     by: New Music Singers, conducted by Graham Treacher

Notes: Composed for Cirencester Grammar School. All the carols are based on mediaeval texts. A record and a tape recording of a performance by the London New Music Singers, conducted by Graham Treacher, is available at the National Sound Archive for private study only.   Note that (iv) is omitted on these recordings.

LEOPARDI FRAGMENTS   (1962)

Catalogue no.:   J53

Descriptive title:	LEOPARDI FRAGMENTS. Cantata for soprano, contralto and ensemble
Musical format:	Voices and instruments
Location of manuscript:	S.A.C. (MS and sketches)
Analysis:	
Performance length:	16 minutes
Composed: 1962	**Revised:**

Instruments: Soprano, Contralto, flute (doubling piccolo), oboe, clarinet, bassoon, trumpet, trombone, harp, cello

Publishing information:	SCHOTT. Full score (36 pp) for sale and hire; parts for hire.
Recording details:	HMV: Record, ASD 640; Record (mono), ALP 2093, ARGO: Record, ZRG 758 and ANGEL: Record, 36387. Mary Thomas (soprano), Rosemary Philips (contralto) and the Melos Ensemble, conducted by John Carewe.
First performance:	July 1962

at: BBC Invitation Concerts at the City of London Festival

by: Dorothy Dorrow (soprano), Rosemary Philips (contralto) and the New Music Ensemble, conducted by John Carewe.

continued ...

Notes: Italian texts from the works of Giacomo Leopardi (1798 - 1837). This was for many years Davies' only setting of non-liturgical words. The work was originally titled *Frammenti di Leopardi*. Manuscript marked "Cirencester 1961". Tape recordings of the first performance, and also of a performance by Jane Manning, Mary Thomas and The Fires of London, conducted by the composer, are available at the National Sound Archive for private study only.

Sir Peter Maxwell Davies.

Roger Lee

LORD'S PRAYER   (1962)

Catalogue no.:   J54

Descriptive title: THE LORD'S PRAYER for SATB chorus

Musical format: Unaccompanied chorus

Location of manuscript:

Analysis:

Performance length: 2 minutes

Composed: 1962   **Revised:**

Instruments: Soprano, Alto, Tenor and Bass chorus

Publishing information: SCHOTT. Score (3 pp) for sale.

Recording details:

First performance: July 1 1962

   at: The opening service of the Cheltenham Festival of British
           Contemporary Music at St. Matthew's Church,
           Cheltenham

   by: Choir of Cirencester Grammar School, conducted by
           the composer

Notes:

SINFONIA   (1962)

Catalogue no.:   J55

Descriptive title: SINFONIA for orchestra

Musical format: Full orchestra

Location of manuscript: Mrs Judy Arnold

Analysis: (i) *Lento recitando* (ii) *Allegro molto moderato* (iii) *Allegro* (iv) *Lento*

Performance length: 20 minutes

Composed: 1962   **Revised:**

Instruments: Flute, oboe, clarinet, bassoon, horn, strings

Publishing information: SCHOTT. Miniature score (41 pp) for sale; full score and parts for hire.

Recording details: UNICORN - KANCHANA: CD, UK(CD) 2026; Cassette, DKP(C) 9058; Record, DKP 9058. Scottish Chamber Orchestra, conducted by the composer.

First performance: May 1982

     at: Royal Festival Hall, London

     by: The English Chamber Orchestra, conducted by Sir Colin Davies

Notes: Commissioned by the English Chamber Orchestra. Tape recordings of performances by the Northern Sinfonia, conducted by Andrew Davies, and by Orchestra Nova of London, conducted by the composer, are available at the National Sound Archive for private study only.

VENI SANCTE SPIRITUS   (1963)

Catalogue no.:   J56

Descriptive title: VENI SANCTE SPIRITUS

Musical format: Voices and orchestra

Location of manuscript: S.A.C. (MS)

Analysis: One continuous movement

Performance length: 20 minutes

Composed: 1963   **Revised:**

Instruments: Soprano, Alto, Tenor and Bass soli, Soprano, Alto, Tenor and Bass chorus, flute, oboe, two bassoons, two horns, two trumpets, two trombones and strings

Publishing information: BOOSEY AND HAWKES.   Full, vocal and choral scores for sale and hire; pocket score for sale only; parts for hire. Full score 47 pp, vocal score 34 pp.

Recording details:

First performance: July 10 1964

   at: Cheltenham Town Hall, Cheltenham Festival

   by: Princeton High School Choir and the English Chamber Orchestra, conducted by Thomas Hilbish

Notes: Tape recordings of the first performance and also of a performance by the BBC Northern Singers and the Northern Sinfonia, conducted by Hall, are available at the National Sound Archive for private study only.

SECOND FANTASIA ON AN 'IN NOMINE' OF JOHN TAVERNER (1964)

Catalogue no.: J57

Descriptive title: SECOND FANTASIA ON AN 'IN NOMINE' OF JOHN TAVERNER

Musical format: Full orchestra

Location of manuscript: S.A.C. (MS "Revised from score"); original pencil MS with Stephen Pruslin

Analysis: 4 movements played continuously

Performance length: 40 minutes

Composed: 1964   **Revised:**

Instruments: Two flutes (second doubling piccolo and alto flute), two oboes (second doubling cor anglais), two clarinets (second doubling bass clarinet), two bassoons (second doubling contrabassoon), four horns, four trumpets, two trombones, two tubas, timpani, harp, strings
Percussion (4 players): side drum, suspended cymbal, tenor drum, bass drum, handbells, glockenspiel, xylophone, tubular bells and tam-tam

Publishing information: BOOSEY AND HAWKES. Pocket score for sale; full score (130 pp) and parts for hire.

Recording details: ARGO: Record, ZRG 712. New Philharmonia Orchestra, conducted by Sir Charles Groves.

continued ...

First performance: 30 April 1965

       at: Royal Festival Hall, London

       by: London Philharmonia Orchestra, conducted by Sir John Pritchard

Notes: Commissioned by the London Philharmonia Orchestra. A tape recording is available at the National Sound Archive for private study only. See also the *Fantasia on an 'In Nomine' of John Taverner* [J51].

MICHAEL PRAETORIUS: CANON (?1964)

Catalogue no.:   J58

Descriptive title: MICHAEL PRAETORIUS: CANON. Realisation of the canon on the frontispiece to the illustrations for *Syntagma Illustrum*, 1619.

Musical format:

Location of manuscript: S.A.C.

Analysis:

Performance length:

Composed: ?1964   **Revised:**

Instruments: No indication

Publishing information: MS (8 pp)

Recording details:

First performance:

      at:

      by:

Notes: Contained in a folder with sketches for *Shakespeare Music* [J59] and jottings for *Ecce Manus* [J64].

SHAKESPEARE MUSIC   (1964)

Catalogue no.:   J59

Descriptive title: SHAKESPEARE MUSIC

Musical format: 11 instrumentalists

Location of manuscript: S.A.C. (MS)

Analysis: (i) Intrada (ii) Pavan (iii) Galliard (iv) Miserere (v) Coranto (vi) Passamezzo (vii) Alman

Performance length: 12 minutes

Composed: 1964   **Revised:**

Instruments: Alto flute (doubling piccolo), oboe, clarinet in A and B flat, bass clarinet in B flat, bassoon (doubling contrabassoon), horn, trombone, guitar, viola, double bass
Percussion (1 player): very small high-pitched wood block, very small high-pitched claves, tabor, very small side drum, tenor drum, very small bass drum, very large bass drum, very small suspended cymbal

Publishing information: BOOSEY AND HAWKES. Full and miniature scores for sale; full score and parts for hire. Full score 36 pp.

Recording details:

First performance: December 8 1964

     at: BBC Invitation Concert, John Lewis Theatre, Oxford Street, London

     by: The Portia Ensemble, conducted by John Carewe

Notes: Commissioned by the BBC for the 400th anniversary of William Shakespeare's birth. A suite of dances from Shakespeare's time. The instruments are used mostly in chamber groupings. Tape recordings of performances by the Portia Ensemble, conducted by John Carewe, and by the Pierrot Players, conducted by the composer, are available at the National Sound Archive for private study only.

AVE, PLENA GRACIA (1964)

Catalogue no.:   J60

Descriptive title: AVE, PLENA GRACIA, carol for SATB chorus with optional organ

Musical format: Unaccompanied chorus/chorus and organ

Location of manuscript: S.A.C. (MS and sketches)

Analysis: No tempo indicated

Performance length: 2 minutes

Composed: 1964   **Revised:**

Instruments: Soprano, Alto, Tenor and Bass, organ optional

Publishing information: OXFORD UNIVERSITY PRESS. Score (8 pp) for sale and hire.

Recording details: ARGO: Record, ZRG 5446; Record (mono), RG 499.   The Elizabethan Singers, conducted by Louis Halsey.

First performance:

at:

by:

Notes: Composed for Cirencester Grammar School.   The above recording is available for private study only at the National Sound Archive.

FIVE LITTLE PIECES FOR PIANO   (1964)

Catalogue no.:   J61

Descriptive title: FIVE LITTLE PIECES FOR PIANO

Musical format: Piano solo

Location of manuscript: S.A.C. (MS)

Analysis: No tempo indicated

Performance length: 5 minutes

Composed: 1964   **Revised:**

Instruments: Piano

Publishing information: BOOSEY AND HAWKES. Score (5 pp) for sale.

Recording details:

First performance: August 1964

   at: Wardour Castle Summer School

   by: The composer, piano

Notes: A tape recording of a performance by Richard Rodney Bennett is available at the National Sound archive for private study only.

THE PAGODA FUGUE   (?1965)

Catalogue no.:   J62

Descriptive title:	THE PAGODA FUGUE
Musical format:	Ten instrumentalists
Location of manuscript:	S.A.C. (MS and sketches)

Analysis: Prelude, Introduction to the Fugue, Fugue I and II, Chorale I and II, Sea Music, Procession, Danse Macabre

Performance length:

Composed: ?1965   **Revised:**

Instruments: Flute (doubling piccolo), oboe, clarinet, bassoon, horn, trumpet in B flat, harp, viola, double bass
Percussion (2 players): *I* - small hand drum (tabor), glockenspiel, small suspended cymbal, electronic effects, side drum with snares and in *Danse Macabre* other percussion ad lib.
II - tam-tam, very large suspended cymbal, very small high woodblock, football rattle and bass drum

Publishing information: MS (26 pp)

Recording details:

First performance:

        at:

        by:

Notes: Incidental music to a BBC play. Sketches in the Archive are marked "Never published nor will be". The date 1965 can be seen in coloured pencils in the sketch. The MS is a copy made for the BBC Music Library (MS 31559).

SEVEN IN NOMINE   (1965)

Catalogue no.:   J63

Descriptive title: SEVEN IN NOMINE

Musical format: 10 instrumentalists

Location of manuscript: S.A.C. (MS and sketches)

Analysis: (i) In Nomine (Taverner/Maxwell Davies) (to the Melos Ensemble) (ii) In Nomine (for Benjamin Britten's 50th birthday) (iii) In Nomine (for Michael Tippett's 60th birthday) (iv) In Nomine (Bull/Maxwell Davies) (v) In Nomine (canon in six parts) (vi) Gloria Tibi Trinitas (Blitheman/Maxwell Davies) (vii) In Nomine (*Lentissimo*)

Performance length: 14 minutes

Composed: 1965   **Revised:**

Instruments: Flute (doubling piccolo), oboe, clarinet, bassoon, horn, harp, violin I, violin II, viola, cello

Publishing information: BOOSEY AND HAWKES. Full score (28 pp) for sale and hire; parts for hire.

Recording details: COLLINS CLASSICS: CD, 10952; Cassette, 10954. Aquarius, conducted by Nicholas Cleobury

First performance: December 3 1965

        at: The Commonwealth Institute, London

        by: Melos Ensemble, conducted by Lawrence Foster

Notes: Commissioned by the Melos Ensemble. The *In Nomine* was a variety of English instrumental music, so called because pieces of this kind were based on the 'in nomine' section of the *Gloria Tibi Trinitas* mass by John Taverner. Tape recordings of performances by the London Sinfonietta, conducted by David Atherton, and the Melos Ensemble, conducted by Lawrence Foster, are available at the National Sound Archive for private study only.

ECCE MANUS TRADENTIS   (1965)

Catalogue no.:   J64

Descriptive title: ECCE MANUS TRADENTIS

Musical format: Voices and instruments

Location of manuscript: S.A.C. (MS and sketches)

Analysis: (i) *Eram quasi agnus* (ii) *In illo tempore*

Performance length: (i) 4 minutes (ii) 20 minutes

Composed: 1965   **Revised:**   1969

Instruments: Soprano, Alto, Tenor and Bass soli, Soprano, Alto, Tenor and Bass chorus, flute, oboe, two bassoons (second doubling contrabassoon), horn, two trombones, harp, handbells (or crotales, C sharp to C sharp)

Publishing information: BOOSEY AND HAWKES. Full score (24 pp) for sale and hire; parts for hire.

Recording details:

First performance: *Eram quasi agnus* June 19 1969; *In illo tempore* August 20 1965

          at: *Eram quasi agnus* Queen Elizabeth Hall, London*; In illo tempore* Wardour Castle Summer School

          by: *Eram quasi agnus* The English Bach Festival Ensemble, conducted by the composer; *In illo Tempore* Bethany Beardsley (soprano), Pauline Stevens (alto), Ian Partridge (tenor), Geoffrey Shaw (bass), the Summer School Choir and the Melos Ensemble, conducted by the composer

Notes: See also *Eram Quasi Agnus* [J84].

REVELATION AND FALL   (1965)

Catalogue no.:   J65

Descriptive title: REVELATION AND FALL: Monodrama
                                for soprano and ensemble

Musical format: Voice(s) and instruments

Location of manuscript: S.A.C. (MS and sketches)

Analysis: One continuous movement

Performance length: 25 minutes

Composed: 1965   **Revised:**   1980

Instruments: Flute (doubling piccolo), clarinet in A (doubling bass clarinet in B flat), bassoon (doubling contrabassoon), horn, trumpet, trombone, harp, two violins, viola, cello, double bass

Percussion (3 players): *I* - glockenspiel, small and large wood blocks, two pebbles, very large ratchet, side drum, tenor drum, very large bass drum, bass drum and cymbal (with foot pedal)

II - glockenspiel, piano (without action), small wood blocks, small claves, large ratchet, very small and large suspended cymbals, metal discs

III - handbells (or crotales) in D flat, small and very large metal claves, two football rattles, two whips, very large bass drum, tam-tam and plastic soapdish, plate glass

Publishing information: BOOSEY AND HAWKES. Full score (84 pp) of both versions for sale; full score and parts of revised version for hire.

continued ...

Recording details: HMV: Record, ASD 2427, and ANGEL: Record, S 36558.   Mary Thomas, soprano and The Pierrot Players, conducted by the composer.

First performance: February 26 1968

     at: A MacNaughton Concert at the Conway Hall, London

     by: Mary Thomas, soprano and The Pierrot Players, conducted by the composer.

Notes: Commissioned for the Serge Koussevitsky Music Foundation in the Library of Congress, Washington, D.C., and dedicated to the memory of Serge and Natalie Koussevitsky.   German text from Georg Trakl's *Offenbarung und Untergang.*   This piece has been described as one of the key works of Davies' expressionism, linking the Austrian Trakl's prose poem with an extreme treatment of Schoenberg's expressionistic style.   A tape recording of the first performance is available at the National Sound Archive for private study only, as are the above recordings.

SHALL I DIE FOR MANNIS SAKE? (1965)

Catalogue no.: J66

Descriptive title: SHALL I DIE FOR MANNIS SAKE? Carol for SA chorus with piano

Musical format: Chorus and piano

Location of manuscript: S.A.C. (Sketches); Ian Kellam (MS)

Analysis: *Andante moderato*

Performance length: 3 minutes

Composed: 1965   **Revised:**

Instruments: Soprano and Alto chorus and piano

Publishing information: BOOSEY AND HAWKES. Score (8 pp) for sale.

Recording details:

First performance:

   at: The London College of Music

   by: The Junior Choir of the London College of Music

Notes:

CANON: I CAN'T COMPOSE TODAY (?1965)

Catalogue no.: J67

Descriptive title: UNTITLED (I Can't Compose Today)

Musical format: No indication

Location of manuscript: S.A.C.

Analysis: No tempo indicated

Performance length:

Composed: ?1965   **Revised:**

Instruments: No indication

Publishing information: MS (1 p)

Recording details:

First performance:

      at:

      by:

Notes: Pencil sketch of a canon on a page containing the sketch of the last bars of *Shall I Die for Mannis Sake?* [J66].

SHEPHERD'S CALENDAR   (1965)

Catalogue no.:   **J68**

Descriptive title: THE SHEPHERD'S CALENDAR for youth chorus (SATB) and ensemble

Musical format: Voice(s) and instruments

Location of manuscript: S.A.C. (MS)

Analysis: (i) *Letabund rediit* (ii) *Vestiunt silve tenera merorem* (iii) *De ramis cadunt folia* (iv) *Veniet Dominus, et non tardabit*

Performance length: 21 minutes

Composed: 1965   **Revised:**

Instruments: Soprano, Alto, Tenor and Bass chorus, flute, oboe, five clarinets, bassoon, trumpet, six recorders, solo string quartet, piano

Percussion (9 players): three side drums, three suspended cymbals, maracas, wood block, two temple blocks, scrubbing board, tam-tam, Japanese jingles, anvil, rattle, tenor drum, small and large bass drums, high wooden and metal claves, two stone discs, two antique cymbals, xylophone, glockenspiel and handbells

Publishing information: BOOSEY AND HAWKES. Full score (33 pp) and parts for sale and hire.

Recording details:

First performance: May 20 1965

at: Sydney, Australia

by: Students of Sydney University and boys of Sydney Church of England Grammar School, conducted by the composer.

Notes: Commissioned by the UNESCO Conference on Music in Education. Texts from the 13th Century Goliard poets. The chorus is doubled throughout by clarinets and bassoons.

NOTRE DAME DES FLEURS (1966)

Catalogue no.:   J69

Descriptive title: NOTRE DAME DES FLEURS

Musical format: Voice(s) and instruments

Location of manuscript: Mrs Judy Arnold (Sketches)

Analysis: One continuous movement

Performance length: 6 minutes

Composed: 1966   **Revised:**

Instruments: Soprano, Mezzo-soprano, Counter-tenor, flute, clarinet in A, piano (doubling celesta), violin, cello
Percussion (1 player): small and large cymbals, triangle, tam-tam, glockenspiel, castanets, wood blocks, bass drum and timpani

Publishing information: CHESTER MUSIC. Miniature score and parts for hire only.

Recording details:

First performance: March 17 1973

    at: Queen Elizabeth Hall, London

    by: Vanessa Redgrave, soprano, Mary Thomas, mezzo-soprano, Grayston Burgess, counter-tenor and The Fires of London, conducted by the composer.

Notes: Text by the composer in obscene French based on the legend of the Virgin and the Unicorn.

FIVE CAROLS   (1966)

Catalogue no.:   J70

Descriptive title: FIVE CAROLS

Musical format: Unaccompanied chorus

Location of manuscript: S.A.C. (MS and sketch)

Analysis: Burden and verses 1 - 5

Performance length: 11 minutes

Composed: 1966   **Revised:**

Instruments: Soprano and Alto chorus

Publishing information: BOOSEY AND HAWKES (7 pp)

Recording details:

First performance: December 11 1966

    at: All Saint's Church, Durham Road, London N2

    by: Finchley Children's Music Group, conducted by John Andrewes

Notes: A tape recording of the first performance is available at the National Sound Archive for private study only.

CANON AD HONOREM I.S.   (1967)

Catalogue no.:   J71

Descriptive title: CANON AD HONOREM I.S.

Musical format: Six voices

Location of manuscript:

Analysis:

Performance length:

Composed: 1967   **Revised:**

Instruments:

Publishing information: MS

Recording details:

First performance:

     at:

     by:

Notes: A tape recording of a performance by the Louis Halsey Singers, conducted by Louis Halsey, is available at the National Sound Archive for private study only.

ANTECHRIST   (1967)

Catalogue no.:   J72

Descriptive title: ANTECHRIST

Musical format: Septet

Location of manuscript: S.A.C.

Analysis: One continuous movement

Performance length: 6 minutes

Composed: 1967   **Revised:**

Instruments: Piccolo, bass clarinet, violin, cello
Percussion (3 players): four handbells (C D E F), four
Burmese gongs (G E C E), cowbell in C, glockenspiel,
tambourine, tabor, tenor drum, bass drum, claves,
Burmese cymbal

Publishing information: BOOSEY AND HAWKES. Full score
(21 pp) and parts for sale.

Recording details: OISEAU-LYRE: Record, DSLO 2. The
Fires of London, conducted by the
composer.

First performance: May 30 1967

        at: Queen Elizabeth Hall, London

        by: Pierrot Players, conducted by the composer

Notes: Written as an overture for the first concert given by the
Fires of London (then the Pierrot Players). Based on a
13th century motet. A record and tape recordings of
performances by the Fires of London, conducted by the
composer, are available at the National Sound Archive for
private study only.

HYMNOS (1967)

Catalogue no.:   J73

Descriptive title: HYMNOS for clarinet and piano
(ΎΜΝΟΣ ᾽ΕΣΠΕΡΙΝΟΣ)

Musical format: Clarinet and piano

Location of manuscript: S.A.C. (MS and sketches)

Analysis: Nine short movements with metronome markings

Performance length: 13 minutes

Composed: 1967   **Revised:**

Instruments: B flat clarinet and piano

Publishing information: BOOSEY AND HAWKES.   Performing score (21 pp) with clarinet part for sale.

Recording details: OISEAU-LYRE: Record, DSLO 2.   Alan Hacker, clarinet and Stephen Pruslin, piano.

First performance: July 1967

at: Cheltenham Town Hall, Cheltenham Festival

by: Alan Hacker, clarinet and Stephen Pruslin, piano

Notes: The above recording is available for private study only at the National Sound Archive.

UNFINISHED SKETCHES II   (1968)

Catalogue no.:   J74

Descriptive title: UNTITLED (Unfinished Sketches II)

Musical format:

Location of manuscript: S.A.C.

Analysis:

Performance length:

Composed: 1968   **Revised:**

Instruments:

Publishing information: MS i: 1 p, ii: 1p, iii: 2pp

Recording details:

First performance:

    at:

    by:

Notes: (i) Opening of a work for two pianos, 1968. Marked 'Machaut. Double Hocket, Triplum'. (ii) Preliminary sketch for a work for two pianos c. 1968 entitled Ἐπιστροφη. (iii) Unfinished realisation of the Machaut work above.

MISSA SUPER L'HOMME ARMÉ   (1968)

Catalogue no.:   J75

Descriptive title: MISSA SUPER L'HOMME ARMÉ for speaker or singer (male or female) and ensemble

Musical format: Voice(s) and instruments

Location of manuscript: S.A.C. (MS and sketches)

Analysis: One continuous movement

Performance length: 20 minutes

Composed: 1968   **Revised:**   1971

Instruments: Flute (doubling piccolo), clarinet in B flat, violin, cello
Keyboards (1 player): harmonium or chamber organ, harpsichord, out-of-tune upright piano and Siamese cymbals
Percussion (1 player): two timpani, side drum, small suspended cymbal, handbells or crotales, large and small tabors, two tin cans, bass drum and cymbal with foot pedal, temple block, swannee whistle, small, medium and large gongs, nightingale, tam-tam, cowbells, tenor drum, wood blocks, small jingles to be played by clarinettist, violinist and cellist

Publishing information: BOOSEY AND HAWKES. Full score (44 pp) for sale and hire; parts for hire.

Recording details: OISEAU-LYRE: Record, DSLO 2. Vanessa Redgrave (speaker) and the Fires of London, conducted by the composer (revised version).

continued ...

First performance: February 26 1968, original version;
                          September 28 1971, revised version,

    at: A MacNaughton Concert at the Conway Hall, London;
                          revised version Sagra Musical Umbra, Perugia

    by: Pierrot Players, conducted by the composer; revised
                          version Murray Melvin and the Fires of London,
                          conducted by the composer

Notes: Called a 'parody mass', this is based on an anonymous
              setting of the *L'Homme Armé* as a mass, which was used
              by several composers in the 15th century. The text is
              from the Vulgate version of St. Luke, chapter 22. The
              original version was written for chamber ensemble with
              electronic tape. A tape recording of the first performance
              of the original version is available at the National Sound
              Archive for private study only, as are a record and a tape
              recording of the revised version with M. Murray and the
              Fires of London, conducted by the composer, and by
              Vanessa Redgrave and the Fires of London, conducted
              by the composer.

STEDMAN CATERS (1968)

Catalogue no.:   J76

Descriptive title: STEDMAN CATERS for ensemble

Musical format: Sextet

Location of manuscript: S.A.C. (MS)

Analysis: Nine movements played continuously: (i) *Lento* (ii) *Allegro moderato* (iii) *Lento molto* (iv) *Lento, rubato* (v) *Moderato* (vi) *Adagio* (vii) *Andante* (viii) *Moderato* (ix) *Lento*

Performance length: 15 minutes

Composed: 1968   **Revised:**

Instruments: Flute (doubling piccolo), clarinet in B flat, harpsichord, viola (doubling wood block and small suspended cymbal), cello (doubling large suspended cymbal) Percussion (1 player): timpani (including 22" timp. to high C), tom-toms or rototoms (for high D and F), handbells (or crotales), tam-tam, glockenspiel, marimba, medium suspended cymbal

Publishing information: BOOSEY AND HAWKES. Full score (19 pp) for sale and hire; parts for hire

Recording details:

First performance: May 30 1968

     at: The Purcell Room, London

     by: Pierrot Players, conducted by the composer

Notes: In change-ringing, *Stedman Caters* is a pattern worked with nine bells. The nine movements are played 'like a succession of points in a ·17th century fantasia', according to the composer. A record and a tape recording of a performance by the Pierrot Players, conducted by the composer, are available at the National Sound Archive for private study only.

PURCELL: FANTASIA ON A GROUND AND TWO PAVANS (1968)

Catalogue no.:   J77

Descriptive title: PURCELL: FANTASIA ON A GROUND AND TWO PAVANS, realisation for ensemble

Musical format: Sextet

Location of manuscript: S.A.C. (MS)

Analysis: (i) Fantasia (ii) Pavans (foxtrots)

Performance length: 12 minutes

Composed: 1968   **Revised:**

Instruments: Piccolo (doubling flute), clarinet in B flat, harpsichord (doubling out-of-tune upright piano), violin, cello
Percussion (1 player): marimba, band kit, optional railway guard's whistle and football rattle

Publishing information: BOOSEY AND HAWKES. Full score (26 pp) for sale and hire; parts for hire.

Recording details: UNICORN - KANCHANA: Record (*Renaissance and Baroque Realisations*), KP 8005; CD, UK CD 2044. The Fires of London, conducted by the composer.

First performance: January 13 1969

at: BBC Concert Hall, Broadcasting House, London

by: Pierrot Players, conducted by the composer

Notes: There is an optional vocal part for the second pavan. A record and a tape recording of the first performance are available at the National Sound Archive for private study only.

SAINT THOMAS WAKE   (1969)

Catalogue no.:   J78

Descriptive title: SAINT THOMAS WAKE. Foxtrot for orchestra on a pavan of John Bull

Musical format: Full orchestra

Location of manuscript: S.A.C. (MS and sketches); S.M.I.C. (preliminary sketches)

Analysis: One continuous movement

Performance length: 20 minutes

Composed: 1969   **Revised:**

Instruments: Piccolo, two flutes, two oboes, two clarinets, bass clarinet, two bassoons, contrabassoon, four horns, three trumpets, three trombones, tuba, timpani, violin, cello, double bass, harp, strings

Percussion (3 players): *I* - Police whistle, side drum, small cymbal, three suspended cymbals, tenor drum, tam-tam, thin metal sheet with hammer, upright piano (no action)

II - two high and two large wood blocks, large biscuit tin filled with glass fragments, football rattle, small bass drum, four metal scaffolding tubes, two hammers

III - referee's whistle, small pair of hard claves, slapstick, large empty biscuit tin, very large bass drum and very small bass drum

Foxtrot Band: piccolo (doubling flute), clarinet, trumpet, trombone

Percussion (1 player): band kit, 'honky-tonk' piano

Publishing information: BOOSEY AND HAWKES. Pocket score for sale; full score (109 pp) and parts for hire.

continued ...

Recording details: LOUISVILLE ORCHESTRA: Record, L 5770. Louisville Orchestra, conducted by Richard Dufallo (available only from Mrs Judy Arnold)

First performance: June 20 1969

at: Dortmund

by: Philharmonia Orchestra of Dortmund, conducted by the composer

Notes: Commissioned by the City of Dortmund. A tape recording of a performance by the Hallé Orchestra, conducted by Sir Alexander Gibson, and a record and a tape recording of a performance by the BBC Symphony Orchestra, conducted by the composer, are available at the National Sound Archive for private study only.

Sir Peter Maxwell Davies at Edinburgh Castle.   Judy Arnold

WORLDES BLIS   (1969)

Catalogue no.:   J79

Descriptive title: WORLDES BLIS: Motet for orchestra

Musical format: Full orchestra

Location of manuscript: S.A.C.

Analysis: One continuous movement

Performance length: 37 minutes

Composed: 1969   **Revised:**

Instruments: Piccolo, two flutes, two oboes, two clarinets, bass
clarinet, two bassoons, double bassoon, four horns, three
trumpets, three trombones, tuba, timpani, two harps,
chamber organ, strings

Percussion (5 players): *I* - woodblock, cymbal, small
suspended cymbal, very small side drum, temple block,
two whips, glockenspiel, xylophone

II - claves, wood block, cymbal, large side drum, temple
block, small anvil, scaffolding struck with metal hammer,
hand bells (or crotales)

III - wood block, cymbal, small and large tam-tam, tenor
drums, tubular bells

IV - bass drum, wood block, cymbal, upright piano (no
action)

V - very large bass drum and cymbal, wood block and
two suspended cymbals

Publishing information: BOOSEY AND HAWKES.   Full score
(151 pp) for sale and hire; parts for hire.

Recording details:

continued ...

First performance: August 28 1969

      at: BBC Promenade Concert, Royal Albert Hall, London

      by: BBC Symphony Orchestra, conducted by the composer

Notes: Commissioned by the BBC for the Promenade Concerts. A tape recording of the first performance is available at the National Sound Archive for private study only.

EIGHT SONGS FOR A MAD KING   (1969)

Catalogue no.:   J80

Descriptive title: EIGHT SONGS FOR A MAD KING. Music-theatre work for baritone (or bass) and ensemble

Musical format: Voice(s) and instruments

Location of manuscript: S.A.C. (MS and sketches)

Analysis: (i) The Sentry (King of Prussia's Minuet) (ii) The Country Walk (La Promenade) (iii) The Lady-in-Waiting (Miss Musgrave's Fancy) (iv) To be sung on the water (The Waterman) (v) The Phantom Queen (He's ay a-kissing me) (vi) The Counterfeit (Le Contre fait) (vii) Country Dance (Scotch Bonnett) (viii) The Review (A Spanish March)

Performance length: 30 minutes

Composed: 1969   **Revised:**

Instruments: Flute (doubling piccolo), clarinet, violin, piano (doubling harpsichord)

Percussion (1 player): side drum, very large and small bass drums, large, regular and small suspended cymbals, foot cymbals, railway whistle, large and small wood blocks, chains, small ratchet, tom-tom, tam-tam, rototoms, tambourine, two temple blocks, toy bird-calls, wind chimes, crotales, very small bells, small steel bars, crow, dijeridu, dulcimer, glockenspiel, small anvil, scrubbing board, squeak, football rattle, band kit

Publishing information: BOOSEY AND HAWKES. Full score (33 pp) for sale and hire; parts for hire.

continued ...

Recording details: UNICORN - KANCHANA: CD, DKP (CD) 9052; Cassette, DKP (C) 9052. Julius Eastman, baritone and the Fires of London, conducted by the composer.
OPUS ONE: Record, 26. John d'Armand, baritone and the Massachusetts University New Music Group, conducted by Charles Fussell.
NONESUCH: Record, H 71285, and UNICORN: Record, UNS 261; Record, RHS 308. Julius Eastman, baritone and the Pierrot Players, conducted by the composer.

First performance: April 22 1969

    at: Queen Elizabeth Hall, London

    by: Roy Hart and the Pierrot Players, conducted by the composer

Notes: Texts by Randolph Stow and King George III. Dedicated to Sir Steven Runciman. A tape recording of the first performance is available at the National Sound Archive for private study only.

CAUDA PAVONIS   (1969)

Catalogue no.:   J81

Descriptive title: CAUDA PAVONIS

Musical format: Piano solo

Location of manuscript:

Analysis:

Performance length:

Composed: 1969   **Revised:**

Instruments: Piano

Publishing information: MS (lost)

Recording details:

First performance: 23 June 1969

      at: The Little Theatre, Bath

      by: The composer, piano

Notes: Advertised as a 'new work based on Schubert's Op.90 No.1' (the Impromptu in C Minor).

SOLITA   (1969)

Catalogue no.:   J82

Descriptive title: SOLITA for flute

Musical format: Flute solo (with musical box)

Location of manuscript: S.M.I.C. (MS and sketches)

Analysis: (i) Introduction (ii) Sonata (iii) *Lento* (iv) *Scherzo* (v) Fugue

Performance length: 8 minutes

Composed: 1969   **Revised:**   1972

Instruments: Flute (and musical box)

Publishing information: BOOSEY AND HAWKES. Score (6 pp) for sale in one volume with *The Kestrel Paced Round the Sun* (10 pp in toto).

Recording details:

First performance: 25 June 1969

     at: York Festival

     by: Judith Pearce, flute

Notes: *Solita* - a little solo and a sonata. The fugue is made possible for solo flute with the addition of the musical box. See also *The Kestrel Paced Round the Sun* [J133].

GABRIELI: CANZONA   (1969)

Catalogue no.:   J83

Descriptive title: GABRIELI: CANZONA. Realisation for
                                chamber ensemble

Musical format: Chamber orchestra

Location of manuscript: Mrs Judy Arnold (parts only)

Analysis: One continuous movement

Performance length: 4 minutes

Composed: 1969   **Revised:**

Instruments: Flute, oboe, clarinet, bassoon, horn and strings

Publishing information: CHESTER MUSIC. Full score for sale
                                and hire; parts for hire.

Recording details:

First performance: 11 April 1969

          at: Queen Elizabeth Hall, London

          by: Orchestra Nova, conducted by the composer

Notes:

ERAM QUASI AGNUS   (1969)

Catalogue no.:   J84

Descriptive title: ERAM QUASI AGNUS

Musical format: Nine instrumentalists

Location of manuscript: S.A.C. (MS and sketches)

Analysis: Instrumental motet

Performance length: 4 minutes

Composed: 1969   **Revised:**

Instruments: Flute, oboe, two bassoons (second doubling contrabassoon), horn, two trombones, harp, handbells (or crotales, C sharp to C sharp)

Publishing information: BOOSEY AND HAWKES. Full score for sale and hire; parts for hire (see *Ecce Manus Tradentis*, [J64]).

Recording details:

First performance: June 19 1969

at: Queen Elizabeth Hall, London

by: English Bach Festival Ensemble, conducted by the composer

Notes: Commissioned by the English Bach Festival. A revision of section (i) of *Ecce Manus Tradentis* [J64].

VESALII ICONES   (1969)

Catalogue no.:   J85

Descriptive title: VESALII ICONES. Music-theatre work for male dancer, solo cello and ensemble.

Musical format: Dancer and ensemble

Location of manuscript: S.A.C. (MS and sketches)

Analysis: (i) The agony in the garden (ii) The betrayal of Judas (iii) Christ before Pilate (iv) The flagellation (v) Christ condemned to death (vi) The mocking of Christ (vii) Christ receives the cross (viii) St. Veronica wipes his face (ix) Christ prepared for death (x) Christ nailed to the cross (xi) The death of Christ (xii) The descent from the cross (xiii) The entombment of Christ (xiv) The resurrection - Antichrist

Performance length: 40 minutes

Composed: 1969   **Revised:**

Instruments: Solo cello, flute (doubling piccolo and alto flute), basset clarinet in A (or clarinet in A), viola, piano (doubling autoharp or zither, cheap commercial tape-recorder, music box, claxon, bamboo blocks, knife and plate), out-of-tune upright piano
Percussion (1 player): glockenspiel, xylophone, small suspended cymbal, band kit, tam-tam, very small wood block, small anvil, sanctus bells, thunder sheet, short lengths of scaffolding, grater, ratchet, whistle, toy clarion, biscuit tin filled with broken glass, chains, manual typewriter, saucepan, two pebbles, blacksmith's bellows

continued ...

Publishing information:	BOOSEY AND HAWKES. Full score (56 pp) for sale and hire; parts and cello and piano reduction for hire.
Recording details:	NONESUCH: Record, H 71295, and UNICORN - KANCHANA: Record, RHS 307; Cassette, RHS (C) 307. Jennifer Ward Clarke, cello and the Fires of London, conducted by the composer.
First performance:	December 9 1969
at:	Queen Elizabeth Hall, London
by:	William Louther, dancer, Jennifer Ward Clarke, cello and the Pierrot Players, conducted by the composer.
Notes:	A balletic counterpoint to the operatic *Eight Songs for a Mad King*. The fourteen linked movements trace a pilgrimage round the Stations of the Cross. The title refers to anatomical drawings of Vesalius. The above recordings and a tape recording of a performance by Jennifer Ward Clarke and the Fires of London, conducted by the composer, are available at the National Sound Archive for private study only.

SUB TUAM PROTECTIONEM   (1969)

Catalogue no.:   J86

Descriptive title: SUB TUAM PROTECTIONEM

Musical format: Piano solo

Location of manuscript: S.A.C. (Sketches); MS with Stephen Pruslin

Analysis: One continuous movement

Performance length: 6 minutes

Composed: 1969   **Revised:**

Instruments: Piano

Publishing information: CHESTER MUSIC. Score (6 pp) for sale in one volume (*Two Piano Pieces*) with *Ut Re Mi* (10 pp in toto).

Recording details:

First performance: 13 January 1970

    at: Purcell Room, London

    by: Stephen Pruslin, piano

Notes: Written for Stephen Pruslin. Fantasy on a motet; the original is a Marian antiphon of Dunstable.

LOST PIECE   (?late 1960s)

Catalogue no.:   **J87**

Descriptive title:	UNTITLED (Lost Piece)
Musical format:	Voice(s) and instruments
Location of manuscript:	S.A.C.
Analysis:	
Performance length:	
Composed: ?late 1960s	**Revised:**
Instruments:	
Publishing information:	MS (6 pp)
Recording details:	
First performance:	
at:	
by:	

Notes: Two copies of a voice part for a song, *O meine müder Füsse*, with indications of orchestration including flute, Siamese cymbals and piano. Undated, probably late 1960s. If the piece should be rediscovered, please inform Mrs Judy Arnold.

NOCTURNAL DANCES   (1969/70)

Catalogue no.:   J88

Descriptive title:	NOCTURNAL DANCES
Musical format:	Ballet
Location of manuscript:	S.A.C. (Sketches)
Analysis:	
Performance length:	
Composed: 1969/70	**Revised:**
Instruments:	
Publishing information:	MS (24 pp)
Recording details:	
First performance:	
at:	
by:	

Notes: Note in archive says '(Abandoned)' but a suite was
made from the dances. The collection is of musical
sketches and correspondence to Barry Moreland of
the London Contemporary Dance Group, for whom
the ballet was to have been written, concerning ideas
for scenes. This is the only remaining sketch, though
Stephen Pruslin may have a set of parts of the suite.

FOUR QUARTETS: INCIDENTAL MUSIC (?1970)

Catalogue no.: J89

Descriptive title: INCIDENTAL MUSIC TO THE 'FOUR QUARTETS' OF T.S. ELIOT

Musical format:

Location of manuscript:

Analysis:

Performance length:

Composed: ?1970 **Revised:**

Instruments:

Publishing information: MS

Recording details:

First performance:

    at:

    by:

Notes: Written for the BBC. The MS is apparently lost, but if it is re-discovered, please send details to Mrs Judy Arnold. A tape recording of a performance by the Fires of London, conducted by the composer, is available at the National Sound Archive for private study only. See also [J101] and [J102] for Machaut arrangements which were apparently written as part of this incidental music.

TAKE A PAIR OF SPARKLING EYES (?1970s)

Catalogue no.:   J90

Descriptive title:	TAKE A PAIR OF SPARKLING EYES: Sullivan, arranged Maxwell Davies
Musical format:	Sextet
Location of manuscript:	S.M.I.C. (MS)
Analysis:	
Performance length:	

Composed: ?1970s   Revised:

Instruments: Flute, B flat clarinet, piano, violin, cello
Percussion (1 player): vibraphone and suspended cymbal

Publishing information: MS (2 pp)

Recording details:

First performance:

at:

by:

Notes: Material at S.M.I.C. includes written-out parts.

WELL   (?1970s)

Catalogue no.:   J91

Descriptive title: THE WELL: INCIDENTAL MUSIC

Musical format: Speakers, voices and ensemble

Location of manuscript: S.M.I.C. (MS and sketch)

Analysis: 8 scenes: (i) The Keeper of the Water - our Island Shore
(ii) Dragon Man (iii) Blessings (iv) The King's Well (v)
Foreigner (vi) Song for a Dry Time (vii) Interview (viii) The
Day of the Long Lead Pipe

Performance length:

Composed: ?1970s   **Revised:**

Instruments: Flute, oboe, clarinet, bassoon, two trumpets, piano, cello,
xylophone
Percussion: tabor (played by pianist), maracas (flautist
and oboist), shaker and tam-tam (bassoonist),
suspended cymbal (pianist)

Publishing information: MS (28 pp)

Recording details:

First performance:

    at:

    by:

Notes: Text by George Mackay Brown. Fair copy of scenes 1
to 8 with sketches for a ninth scene.

TAVERNER   (1970)

Catalogue no.:   J92

Descriptive title:	TAVERNER. Opera in 2 acts
Musical format:	Opera
Location of manuscript:	S.A.C. (MS, sketches and notes)

Analysis: Act I: Scene 1, A courtroom; Scene 2, The chapel; Scene 3, The throne room; Scene 4, the same. Act II: Scene 1, The courtroom; Scene 2, The throne room; Scene 3, The chapel; Scene 4, The market-place in Boston, Lincolnshire.

Performance length: 130 minutes

Composed: 1970   **Revised:**

Instruments: *Pit orchestra*: Two flutes (doubling piccolo), two oboes (second doubling cor anglais), clarinet in A and B flat doubling E flat, clarinet in B flat doubling E flat and bass clarinet, two bassoons (second doubling contrabassoon), four horns in F, four trumpets in C (third and fourth doubling piccolo trumpets in F off stage), two trombones, two tubas, timpani, harmonium, harp, strings
Percussion (5 players): glockenspiel, tubular bells, small French cowbell, Japanese jingles, metal disc, knife and grinding wheel, high metal and very high wood claves, small and very large maracas, wood block, four temple blocks, castanet machine, football rattle, large ratchet, very small and large tambourines, very small and medium side drums, tabor, tenor drum, small, medium and very large bass drums, small Turkish cymbal, pair of cymbals, small, large and very large suspended cymbals, very large cracked cymbal, tam-tam, very large and heavy coil bell, upright piano (no action), six handbells, five deep tuned gongs, small and large church bells

continued ...

page 104

On-stage instruments: Lute, tenor viols I and 2, bass viols 1, 2, 3 and 4, violone, two soprano shawms (one doubling alto shawm), tabor, side drum, sopranino recorder, cornett in C (or sopranino shawm), bass shawm (or two serpents), alto trombone (or sackbutt), nakers (A,C), positive organ, regal, twelve soldiers' drums

Publishing information: BOOSEY AND HAWKES. Pocket score and libretto for sale; vocal score for sale and hire; full score (379 pp) and parts for hire.

Recording details:

First performance: July 12 1972

at: Royal Opera House, Covent Garden

by: R. Ulfung, tenor, G. Howell, bass, J. Lanigan, tenor, N. Mangin, bass, B. Luxon, baritone, R. Herincx, bass-baritone, J. Bowman, counter-tenor and the Covent Garden Orchestra, conducted by Edward Downes. Produced by Michael Goliot and designed by Ralph Koltai

Notes: Libretto by the composer from documents of the 16th century. Piano reduction for the vocal score by Stephen Pruslin. The first sketches were made in 1956; the text was completed in 1962 and the music in 1968, though some of this was reworked after a fire at the composer's cottage. A tape recording of the Covent Garden performance is available at the National Sound Archive for private study only.

POINTS AND DANCES FROM 'TAVERNER' (1970)

Catalogue no.:	**J93**
Descriptive title:	POINTS AND DANCES FROM 'TAVERNER'. Instrumental dances and keyboard pieces from the opera.
Musical format:	Act I: Sextet, Act II: Octet
Location of manuscript:	S.A.C. (MS of Act I)
Analysis:	From Act I: (i) Pavan (ii) Galliard (iii) March From Act II: (i) Intrada (ii) Preambulum (iii) Pavan (iv) *Miserere* (v) Galliard (vi) *Te per orbem terrarum* (vii) Dumpe (viii) *Eterne rex altissime* (ix) *Eterne rex alia* (x) *Eterne rerum conditor* (xi) Corant
Performance length:	18 minutes
Composed: 1970	**Revised:**
Instruments:	*Act I*: Alto flute, clarinet, harpsichord, guitar, viola and cello; *Act II*: Piccolo, clarinet, contrabassoon, trumpet, alto trombone, regal, positive organ Percussion (1 player): pair of small tuned drums
Publishing information:	BOOSEY AND HAWKES. Miniature score of *Points and dances from Act II* for sale; full score (40 pp) and parts for hire.
Recording details:	ARGO: Record, ZRG 712. The Fires of London, conducted by the composer.
First performance:	February 20 1971
at:	Queen Elizabeth Hall, London
by:	The Fires of London, conducted by the composer
Notes:	A tape recording of the first performance is available at the National Sound Archive for private study only.

UT RE MI   (1970)

Catalogue no.:   J94

Descriptive title: UT RE MI

Musical format: Piano solo

Location of manuscript: S.A.C. (sketch); MS with Stephen
                                Pruslin

Analysis: (i) *Moderato* (ii) *Lento* (iii) *Allegro*

Performance length: 3 minutes

Composed: 1970   **Revised:**

Instruments: Piano

Publishing information: CHESTER MUSIC. Score (3 pp) for
                                sale in one volume (*Two Piano
                                Pieces*) with *Sub Tuam Protectionem*
                                (10 pp in toto).

Recording details:

First performance: January 19 1971

    at: Purcell Room, London

    by: Stephen Pruslin, piano

Notes: Written for Stephen Pruslin

BUXTEHUDE: ALSO HAT GOTT DIE WELT GELIEBET (1970)

Catalogue no.:   J95

Descriptive title: BUXTEHUDE: ALSO HAT GOTT DIE WELT GELIEBET. Cantata for soprano and ensemble; realisation including 'original' interpretation.

Musical format: Voice(s) and instruments

Location of manuscript:

Analysis: One continuous movement

Performance length: 12 minutes

Composed: 1970   **Revised:**

Instruments: Soprano, flute, harpsichord (doubling celesta), violin, cello

Publishing information: CHESTER MUSIC. Full score (16 pp) and parts on sale separately.

Recording details:

First performance: August 10 1970

          at: Dartington Summer School

          by: Mary Thomas (soprano) and the Pierrot Players, conducted by the composer

Notes: A tape recording of a performance by Mary Thomas and The Fires of London, conducted by the composer, is available at the National Sound Archive for private study only.

FROM STONE TO THORN   (1971)

Catalogue no.:   **J96**

Descriptive title: FROM STONE TO THORN for mezzo-soprano and ensemble

Musical format: Voice(s) and instruments

Location of manuscript: Mrs Sylvia Junge

Analysis: One continuous movement

Performance length: 13 minutes

Composed: 1971   **Revised:**

Instruments: Mezzo-soprano, clarinet in A (or basset clarinet in A), harpsichord, guitar
Percussion (1 player): glockenspiel, coiled spring, very small, small and large temple blocks, very small and small wood block, bell tree, small, large and very large cymbals, wind chimes, tam-tam, small bass drum, flexatone

Publishing information: BOOSEY AND HAWKES. Full score (20 pp) for sale and hire; parts for hire.

Recording details: OISEAU-LYRE: Record, DSLO 2. Mary Thomas (mezzo-soprano) and the Fires of London, conducted by the composer.

continued ...

First performance: June 30 1971

    at: Holywell Music Room, Oxford

    by: Mary Thomas (mezzo-soprano), Alan Hacker (clarinet), Stephen Pruslin (harpsichord), Timothy Walker (guitar) and Barry Quinn (percussion), conducted by the composer

Notes: Commissioned by Jesus College, Oxford, for its four hundredth anniversary. This is Davies' first Orkney piece. The text is by George Mackay Brown from the poem-cycle *Fishermen with Ploughs*. The above recording is available for private study at the National Sound Archive.

BELL TOWER   (1971)

Catalogue no.:   J97

Descriptive title: BELL TOWER (*Turris Campanum Sonantium*) for percussion

Musical format: Percussion

Location of manuscript: Unknown

Analysis: Unknown

Performance length:

Composed: 1971   **Revised:**

Instruments: Unknown

Publishing information: MS - lost

Recording details: OISEAU-LYRE: Record, DSLO 1. Stomu Yamash'ta, percussion.

First performance:

    at:

    by:

Notes: Written for Stomu Yamash'ta. Withdrawn by the composer; nothing remains of this piece to his knowledge. A copy of the above recording is available at the National Sound Archive for private study only.

SUITE FROM 'THE DEVILS'   (1971)

Catalogue no.:   J98

Descriptive title: SUITE FROM 'THE DEVILS' for instrumental ensemble with soprano obligato; drawn from the soundtrack of Ken Russell's film.

Musical format: Voice(s) and instruments

Location of manuscript: S.M.I.C. (MS and sketch)

Analysis:

Performance length: 25 minutes

Composed: 1971   **Revised:**

Instruments: Soprano, flute (doubling alto flute and piccolo), clarinet (doubling bass clarinet), trumpet, trombone, Hammond organ (doubling out-of-tune upright piano and celesta), violin (doubling viola and regal organ), cello, double bass

Percussion (3 players): *I* - timpani, four suspended cymbals, temple gong, four wood blocks, chains, bamboo whistle, foxtrot kit, thunder sheet, tam-tam, large tabor, tambourine, Indian temple jingles

II - marimba, small suspended Chinese cymbal, flexatone, lion's roar, tam-tam, grater, small bass drum, untuned zither, nightingale, rubber plunger in water, large bass drum, cycle wheel

III - thunder sheet, four suspended cymbals, four pieces of scaffolding, small bass drum, grater, blackboard (scraped with fingernails), knife and plate, upright piano, tam-tam

Publishing information: CHESTER MUSIC. Full score (65 pp) and parts for hire only.

continued ...

Recording details: COLLINS CLASSICS: CD, 10952; Cassette, 10954. Aquarius, conducted by Nicholas Cleobury.

First performance: December 11 1971

     at: Queen Elizabeth Hall, London

     by: The Fires of London, conducted by the composer

Notes: Drawn from the soundtrack of Ken Russell's film *The Devils*. A tape recording of the first performance is available at the National Sound Archive for private study only.

SUITE FROM 'THE BOYFRIEND'   (1971)

Catalogue no.:   **J99**

Descriptive title: SUITE FROM 'THE BOYFRIEND' for small orchestra; drawn from the sound track of Ken Russell's film based on the musical by Sandy Wilson

Musical format: Full orchestra

Location of manuscript: S.M.I.C. (MS and sketch)

Analysis: (i) Introduction - The Boy Friend - I could be happy with you (ii) Sur la Plage (iii) A room in Bloomsbury (iv) I could be happy with you (v) The you don't want to play with me blues (vi) Poor little Pierrette (vii) Polly's dream

Performance length: 25 minutes

Composed: 1971   **Revised:**

Instruments: Two clarinets (first doubling bass clarinet), soprano saxophone (doubling alto saxophone and soprano saxophone or E flat clarinet), alto saxophone (doubling tenor saxophone), tenor saxophone, two trumpets, trombone, tuba, timpani, strings, tenor banjo, ukulele (doubling mandolin), harp

Percussion (2 players): Dance band kit (including side drum, bass drum, cymbals, four temple blocks, wood blocks and scrubbing boards), vibraphone, xylophone, glockenspiel, tubular bells, jingles, swannee whistles, nightingale, cuckoo effect, duck effect, güiro, tambourine, crotales and tam-tam (with plastic soap dish)

Keyboards (2 players): piano duet (right-hand player doubling celesta and autoharp, left-hand player doubling tambourine and requiring scrape for inside the piano)

continued ...

Publishing information:	CHESTER MUSIC. Full score (161 pp) and parts for hire only.
Recording details:	COLLINS CLASSICS: CD, 10952; Cassette, 10954. Aquarius, conducted by Nicholas Cleobury.
First performance:	December 11 1971
at:	Queen Elizabeth Hall, London
by:	The Fires of London, conducted by the composer
Notes:	Manuscript material is also in the possession of Gerard McBurney, who wrote out the score of the suite. A tape recording of the first performance is available at the National Sound Archive for private study only.

Sir Peter Maxwell Davies at his home at Hoy, Orkney Islands
Ros Drinkwater — The Sunday Times

PUSSYCAT   (?1971)

Catalogue no.:   J100

Descriptive title: UNTITLED (PUSSY CAT)
Musical format: Voice and piano
Location of manuscript: Gerard McBurney
Analysis: Two parts; no tempo indicated
Performance length:
Composed: ?1971   **Revised:**
Instruments: "Heldentenor und Grosses Hammerklavier"
Publishing information: MS
Recording details:
First performance:
    at:
    by:
Notes: A short piece written for Gerard McBurney, who wrote
                 out the score of the Suite from *The Boy Friend*. See also
                 Cantata Profunda Op. 2002 [J152] for another
                 light-hearted setting of the same words.

page 116

MACHAUT: HOQUETUS DAVID (1971)

Catalogue no.: J101

Descriptive title: HOQUETUS DAVID: Machaut, arranged Maxwell Davies

Musical format: Soprano and ensemble

Location of manuscript:

Analysis:

Performance length:

Composed: 1971 **Revised:**

Instruments:

Publishing information:

Recording details:

First performance:

at:

by:

Notes: A tape recording is available at the National Sound archive for private study only. The piece is part of the *Four Quartets* incidental musc [J89].

MACHAUT: MA FIN EST
MON COMMENCEMENT   (1971)

Catalogue no.:   J102

Descriptive title: MA FIN EST MON COMMENCEMENT:
                                  Machaut, arranged Maxwell Davies

Musical format: Instrumental ensemble

Location of manuscript:

Analysis:

Performance length:

Composed: 1971   **Revised:**

Instruments:

Publishing information: MS

Recording details:

First performance:

       at:

       by:

Notes: A tape recording of a performance by the Fires of London
                   is available at the National Sound Archive for private
                   study only.   The piece is possibly part of the *Four
                   Quartets* incidental music.

SONG (UNPUBLISHED)   (?1972)

Catalogue no.:   J103

Descriptive title: SONG (UNPUBLISHED)

Musical format: Voice (treble clef) and guitar

Location of manuscript: S.M.I.C.

Analysis: *Lento recitando*

Performance length:

Composed: ?1972   **Revised:**

Instruments: Voice and guitar

Publishing information: MS (1 p)

Recording details:

First performance:

    at:

    by:

Notes: At the foot of the song is written *"The Winter's Task* by Robert Wells, published by Carcanet Press (Manchester)", but the MS is bound with material marked "Unpublished Song 1972.   George Mackay Brown."

SKETCH I   (?1972)

Catalogue no.:   J104

Descriptive title: SKETCH I (UNTITLED)

Musical format: Alto flute and marimba

Location of manuscript: S.M.I.C. (sketch)

Analysis: No tempo indicated

Performance length:

Composed: ?1972   **Revised:**

Instruments: Alto flute, marimba

Publishing information: MS (1 p)

Recording details:

First performance:

      at:

      by:

Notes: Undated, but with other unpublished material dating
from 1972.

WALTON TRIBUTE   (1972)

Catalogue no.:   J105

Descriptive title: WALTON TRIBUTE

Musical format: Full orchestra

Location of manuscript: S.M.I.C. (MS and sketch)

Analysis: *Alla marcia - andante*

Performance length:

Composed: 1972   **Revised:**

Instruments: Piccolo, flute, two oboes, two clarinets, two bassoons, four horns, three trumpets, two trombones, tuba, timpani, strings
Percussion: cymbal and tambourine

Publishing information: MS (2 pp)

Recording details:

First performance:

     at:

     by:

Notes: Written for Sir William Walton's 70th birthday, March 1972.

BLIND MAN'S BUFF   (1972)

Catalogue no.:   J106

Descriptive title:	BLIND MAN'S BUFF. Masque for soprano (or treble), mezzo-soprano, mime and small orchestra.
Musical format:	Voice(s) and instruments
Location of manuscript:	S.M.I.C. (MS and sketch)

Analysis: Masque

Performance length: 20 minutes

Composed: 1972   **Revised:**

Instruments: Soprano (or Treble), Mezzo-soprano
Stage band: Flute (doubling piccolo and alto flute), clarinet in A, horn, guitar (doubling tenor banjo), ukulele (doubling mandolin), harp
Percussion (1 player): side drum, tenor drum, bass drum and cymbal (foot-operated), two cymbals (suspended), glockenspiel, four crotales, bell tree, wood block, temple block, güiro, claves
Pit orchestra: Four first violins, four second violins, three violas, three cellos, double bass

Publishing information: CHESTER MUSIC. Full score (46 pp) for sale and hire; parts for hire.

Recording details:

continued ...

First performance: May 29 1972

   at: The Round House, Camden, London

   by: Josephine Barstow (soprano), Mary Thomas
            (mezzo-soprano), Mark Furneaux (mime) and the BBC
            Symphony Orchestra, conducted by Pierre Boulez

Notes: Commissioned by the BBC. Text by the composer
            from the last scene of Büchner's *Leonce und Lena*
            and English nursery rhymes. A tape recording of the
            first performance is available at the National Sound
            Archive for private study only.

FOOL'S FANFARE   (1972)

Catalogue no.:   J107

Descriptive title:	FOOL'S FANFARE for speaker and ensemble
Musical format:	Voice(s) and instruments
Location of manuscript:	S.M.I.C. (MS and sketch)
Analysis:	One continuous movement
Performance length:	7 minutes
Composed: 1972	**Revised:**

Instruments: Two trumpets, two trombones, ukulele (doubling mandolin)
Percussion (2 players): *I* - glockenspiel, large and small choke cymbals, tambourine, four timpani
II - marimba, four temple blocks, four wood blocks

Publishing information: CHESTER MUSIC Full score (8 pp) for sale and hire; parts for hire.

Recording details:

First performance: April 23 1972

at: Southwark Cathedral, London

by: Ron Moody (speaker) and the London Sinfonietta, conducted by the composer

Notes: Commissioned by the Globe Playhouse Trust Ltd. A realisation of Shakespeare's fools, with texts drawn from *King Lear*, *A Midsummer Night's Dream*, *Hamlet* and *As You Like It*.

HYMN TO ST. MAGNUS   (1972)

Catalogue no.:   J108

Descriptive title: HYMN TO ST. MAGNUS for ensemble
                                with mezzo-soprano obbligato

Musical format: Voice(s) and instruments

Location of manuscript: S.M.I.C. (MS)

Analysis: (i) *Adagio* (ii) *Moderato* (iii) *Andante* (iv) *Lento*
                       (played without a break)

Performance length: 37 minutes

Composed: 1972   **Revised:**

Instruments: Mezzo-soprano, flute, clarinet in A (or basset clarinet in
                   A), piano (doubling harpsichord and celesta), viola, cello
                   Percussion (1 player): timpani, glockenspiel, marimba,
                   crotales, small Chinese cymbal, six nipple gongs, four
                   large bells, tam-tam, small suspended cymbal, bass drum
                   and cymbal with foot pedal, handbells

Publishing information: BOOSEY AND HAWKES. Full score
                                (89 pp) for sale and hire; parts for
                                hire.

Recording details: OISEAU-LYRE: Record, DSLO 12.
                                Mary Thomas, mezzo- soprano and the
                                Fires of London, conducted by the
                                composer.

continued ...

First performance: October 13 1972

      at: Queen Elizabeth Hall, London

      by: Mary Thomas, mezzo-soprano and the Fires of London, conducted by the composer

Notes: Magnus was a 12th century Earl of Orkney who was murdered by his cousin and became revered as a martyr. The central movements are in sonata form, the opening movement a short introduction and the closing a setting of the mediaeval hymn to St. Magnus. The above recording is available for private study only at the National Sound Archive.

TENEBRAE SUPER GESUALDO   (1972)

Catalogue no.:   J109

Descriptive title: TENEBRAE SUPER GESUALDO for
mezzo-soprano, guitar and
instrumental ensemble

Musical format: Voice(s) and instruments

Location of manuscript: S.M.I.C. (MS and sketch)

Analysis: One continuous movement in seven sections

Performance length: 20 minutes

Composed: 1972   **Revised:**

Instruments: Mezzo-soprano, alto flute, bass clarinet, marimba
(doubling glockenspiel), harpsichord (doubling celesta
and chamber organ or harmonium), violin (doubling
viola), cello, guitar (accompanying mezzo-soprano)

Publishing information: CHESTER MUSIC. Full score (18 pp)
for sale and hire; parts for hire.

Recording details: UNICORN-KANCHANA: Record, KP
8002; CD, UKCD 2044. Mary Thomas
(mezzo-soprano), Timothy Walker
(guitar) and the Fires of London,
conducted by the composer.

First performance: August 25 1972

      at: A South Bank Summer Music concert at the Queen
Elizabeth Hall, London

      by: Mary Thomas (mezzo-soprano), Timothy Walker (guitar)
and the Fires of London, conducted by the composer

Notes: See also [J110].

TENEBRAE SUPER GESUALDO   (1972)

Catalogue no.:   J110

Descriptive title:	TENEBRAE SUPER GESUALDO for ensemble and SATB choir
Musical format:	Voice(s) and instruments
Location of manuscript:	S.M.I.C. (MS and sketch)

Analysis: One continuous movement in seven sections

Performance length: 20 minutes

Composed: 1972   **Revised:**

Instruments: Soprano, Alto, Tenor and Bass choir, alto flute, bass clarinet, marimba (doubling glockenspiel), harpsichord (doubling celesta and chamber organ or harmonium), violin (doubling viola), cello

Publishing information: CHESTER MUSIC. Full score (18 pp) for sale and hire; parts for hire.

Recording details:

First performance: January 28 1982

    at: St. James, Piccadilly, London

    by: The Music Ensemble and the Music Ensemble Chorus, conducted by Keith Williams

Notes: See also [J109].

CANON IN MEMORIAM IGOR STRAVINSKY (1971)

Catalogue no.: J111

Descriptive title: CANON IN MEMORIAM IGOR STRAVINSKY.

Musical format: Puzzle canon

Location of manuscript: S.M.I.C. (MS)

Analysis: Puzzle canon

Performance length: Variable

Composed: 1971 **Revised:**

Instruments: Flute, clarinet, harp and string quartet

Publishing information: BOOSEY AND HAWKES. Full score for hire. Score published in *Tempo* No.97, 1971.

Recording details:

First performance: Broadcast: April 6 1972
Public: June 17 1972

at: Broadcast: BBC Radio 3
Public:St John's Smith Square, London

by: Broadcast: The Vesuvius Ensemble
Public:The London Sinfonietta

Notes: Commissioned for the journal *Tempo* to be part of a collection of epitaphs. A solution to this puzzle canon was published in *Tempo* No. 100, 1972.

LULLABYE FOR ILIAN RAINBOW   (1972)

Catalogue no.:   J112

Descriptive title: LULLABYE FOR ILIAN RAINBOW

Musical format: Guitar solo

Location of manuscript: S.M.I.C. (MS)

Analysis: (i) Lullaby (ii) Double (iii) Toccata (iv) Lullaby II

Performance length: 5 minutes

Composed: 1972   **Revised:**

Instruments: Guitar

Publishing information: BOOSEY AND HAWKES. Score (6 pp) for sale.

Recording details: OISEAU-LYRE: Record, DSLO 3. Timothy Walker, guitar.

First performance: September 18 1972

    at: Queen Elizabeth Hall, London

    by: Timothy Walker, guitar

Notes: Composed for the birth of guitarist Timothy Walker's son. The above recording is available for private study only at the National Sound Archive.

J.S. BACH: PRELUDE AND FUGUE IN C SHARP MINOR (1972)

Catalogue no.: J113

Descriptive title: J.S. BACH: PRELUDE AND FUGUE IN C SHARP MINOR, the '48', Book I. Realisation for ensemble

Musical format: Sextet

Location of manuscript: S.M.I.C. (sketch)

Analysis: Prelude: *Andante expressivo* Fugue: *Molto moderato e maestoso*

Performance length: 5 minutes

Composed: 1972 **Revised:**

Instruments: Flute (doubling alto flute), clarinet in A, harpsichord, marimba, viola and cello

Publishing information: BOOSEY AND HAWKES. Full score (32 pp) for sale (in one volume with the *Prelude and fugue in C sharp major*) and hire; parts for hire.

Recording details: UNICORN-KANCHANA: Record, *Renaissance and Baroque Realisations* KP 8005; CD, UKCD 2044. The Fires of London, conducted by the composer.

First performance: October 13 1972

at: Queen Elizabeth Hall, London

by: The Fires of London, conducted by the composer

Notes: A tape recording of a performance by The Fires of London is available at the National Sound Archive for private study only. See also [J125].

DUNSTABLE: VENI SANCTE SPIRITUS - VENI CREATOR SPIRITUS

(1972)

Catalogue no.:   J114

Descriptive title: DUNSTABLE: VENI SANCTE SPIRITUS
- VENI CREATOR SPIRITUS. Realisation
plus original work, for ensemble

Musical format: Sextet

Location of manuscript: Boosey and Hawkes

Analysis: (i) *Veni sancte spiritus* (ii) *Veni creator spiritus*

Performance length: 9 minutes

Composed: 1972   **Revised:**

Instruments: Alto flute, clarinet in A, glockenspiel, harpsichord
(doubling piano), viola, cello

Publishing information: BOOSEY AND HAWKES. Full score
(22 pp) for sale and hire; parts for
hire.

Recording details: UNICORN-KANCHANA: Record,
Renaissance and Baroque Realisations
KP 8005; CD, UKCD 2044. The Fires of
London, conducted by the composer.

First performance: May 6 1972

at: Queen Elizabeth Hall, London

by: The Fires of London, conducted by the composer

Notes: *Veni sancte spiritus* is a realisation of the Dunstable
motet. *Veni creator spiritus* is taken as the point of
departure for an original fantasy.

STONE LITANY - RUNES FROM A HOUSE OF THE DEAD (1973)

Catalogue no.:   J115

Descriptive title: STONE LITANY - RUNES FROM A HOUSE OF THE DEAD for mezzo-soprano and orchestra

Musical format: Mezzo-soprano and orchestra

Location of manuscript: S.M.I.C. (MS and sketches)

Analysis: One continuous movement

Performance length: 20 minutes

Composed: 1973   **Revised:**

Instruments: Piccolo, flute, clarinet, bass clarinet (doubling E flat clarinet), bassoon, contrabassoon, two horns, two trumpets, two trombones, tuba, timpani, harp, celeste, strings

Percussion: (5 players): Glockenspiel, marimba, flexatone, two wine or brandy glasses (E flat and C), crotales, bell tree, two wood blocks, two temple blocks, two maracas, tabor, rototoms, bass drum, three nipple gongs (G sharp, E, C), tubular bells, Chinese cymbal, small suspended cymbal (with double bass bow), anvil, tam-tam

Publishing information: BOOSEY AND HAWKES. Pocket score for sale; full score (75 pp) and parts for hire.

Recording details:

continued ...

First performance: September 22 1973

         at: City Hall, Glasgow

         by: Jan DeGaetani (mezzo-soprano) and the Scottish National Orchestra, conducted by Sir Alexander Gibson

Notes: Commissioned by the Scottish National Orchestra and the University of Glasgow for Musica Nova. The text is from Viking runic inscriptions in Maes-howe tomb, Orkney. Tape recordings of the first performance, and also of a performance by Jane Manning and the BBC Scottish Symphony Orchestra, conducted by Christopher Seaman, are available at the National Sound Archive for private study only.

RENAISSANCE SCOTTISH DANCES

(1973)

Catalogue no.:   J116

Descriptive title: RENAISSANCE SCOTTISH DANCES for ensemble (Anon.: arranged Maxwell Davies)

Musical format: Sextet

Location of manuscript: S.M.I.C. (MS)

Analysis: (i) Intrada (ii) Currant (iii) Sweit smylling Katie loves me (with Ladie Louthian's Lilte) (iv) Last time I came over the Mure (v) Ane Exempill of Tripla (vi) Remember me my dear (vii) Almayne

Performance length: 9 minutes

Composed: 1973   **Revised:**

Instruments: Flute, clarinet (optionally doubling clarinet in C), guitar, violin, cello

Percussion (1 player): glockenspiel (or other tuned percussion), marimba (or bass xylophone), tambourine, bunch of keys (or dried peas in a tin), two woodblocks (see Notes)

Publishing information: BOOSEY AND HAWKES. Full score (11 pp) and parts for sale and hire.

Recording details: UNICORN-KANCHANA: *A Celebration of Scotland*; CD, DKP (CD) 9070; Cassette, DKP (C) 9070. Members of the Scottish Chamber Orchestra, conducted by the composer.

OISEAU-LYRE: Record, DLSO 12. The Fires of London, conducted by the composer

continued ...

First performance: July 29 1973

      at: Dartington Summer Festival

      by: The Fires of London, conducted by the composer

Notes: The instrumentation may be adapted to individual requirements, e.g. the guitar part could be played on the harpsichord and the wind parts played on alternative instruments. The above recordings are available for private study at the National Sound Archive.

SI QUIS DILIGET ME   (1973)

Catalogue no.:   J117

Descriptive title: SI QUIS DILIGET ME. Motet for ensemble. Peebles and Heagy, arranged Maxwell Davies.

Musical format: Sextet

Location of manuscript: Boosey and Hawkes

Analysis: One continuous movement

Performance length: 4 minutes

Composed: 1973   **Revised:**

Instruments: Alto flute, clarinet in B flat, celesta, crotales, viola, cello

Publishing information: BOOSEY AND HAWKES. Full score (27 pp) for sale (in the volume *Four instrumental motets*); full score and parts for hire.

Recording details: UNICORN-KANCHANA: Record, *Renaissance and Baroque Realisations* KP 8005; CD, UKCD 2044. The Fires of London, conducted by the composer.

First performance: July 29 1973

at: Dartington Summer School

by: The Fires of London, conducted by the composer

Notes: The first of four 'instrumental motets' based on music of the 16th century Scottish church. See also *All sons of Adam*, 1974 [J122], *Our Father whiche in Heaven art*, 1977 [J151] and *Psalm 124*, 1974 [J123]. Unlike the other motets, it is a straight transcription. A tape recording is available at the National Sound Archive for private study only.

PURCELL: FANTASIA ON ONE NOTE (1973)

Catalogue no.:   J118

Descriptive title: PURCELL: FANTASIA ON ONE NOTE.
Realisation for ensemble

Musical format: Sextet

Location of manuscript: S.M.I.C. (MS)

Analysis: One continuous movement

Performance length: 5 minutes

Composed: 1973   **Revised:**

Instruments: Alto flute, basset clarinet in A (or clarinet in A), harpsichord (doubling brandy glass and cello, one note), violin (doubling harpsichord), cello
Percussion (1 player): marimba, crotales, banjo, rototoms

Publishing information: CHESTER MUSIC. Full score (7 pp) for sale and hire; parts for sale.

Recording details: UNICORN-KANCHANA: Record, *Renaissance and Baroque Realisations* KP 8005. The Fires of London, conducted by the composer.

First performance: July 24 1973

at: A BBC Promenade Concert at the Royal Albert Hall, London

by: The Fires of London, conducted by the composer

Notes: A tape recording of the first performance is available for private study at the National Sound Archive.

FIDDLERS AT THE WEDDING   (1973)

Catalogue no.:   J119

Descriptive title:	FIDDLERS AT THE WEDDING for mezzo-soprano and ensemble
Musical format:	Voice(s) and instruments
Location of manuscript:	S.M.I.C. (MS and sketch)
Analysis:	(i) Fiddlers at the wedding (ii) Interlude (iii) Ikey's Day (iv) Interlude (v) Roads (vi) Interlude (vii) Peat Cutting
Performance length:	19 minutes
Composed: 1973 **Revised:**	
Instruments:	Mezzo-soprano, alto flute, mandolin, guitar
	Percussion (1 player): five glass brandy bowls placed on medium pedal timpani, very small bongo or pottery drum, marimba, crotales, Chinese cymbal, deep nipple gong, bell tree, small wood block, glass wind chimes, sandpaper block
Publishing information:	BOOSEY AND HAWKES. Full score (16 pp) for sale and hire; parts for hire
Recording details:	
First performance:	May 3 1974
at:	Salle Pleyel, Paris
by:	Jane Manning (mezzo-soprano) and the Ensemble Instrumental, conducted by Daniel Chabrun
Notes:	Text by George Mackay Brown from the poem-cycle *Fishermen with Ploughs.* A tape recording is available at the National Sound Archive for private study only.

PSALM 124 (1974)

Catalogue no.:   J123

Descriptive title: PSALM 124. Motet for ensemble. Peebles, Fethy, Anon., arranged Maxwell Davies.

Musical format: Septet

Location of manuscript: S.M.I.C. (MS)

Analysis: Three motet realisations

Performance length: 10 minutes

Composed: 1974   **Revised:**

Instruments: Flute (doubling alto flute), bass clarinet, guitar, violin (doubling viola), cello, glockenspiel and marimba

Publishing information: BOOSEY AND HAWKES. Full score (27pp) for sale in the volume *Four Instrumental Motets*; full score and parts for hire.

Recording details: OISEAU-LYRE: Record, DSLO 12. The Fires of London, conducted by the composer.

First performance: July 28 1974

at: Dartington Summer School

by: The Fires of London, conducted by the composer

Notes: One of four 'instrumental motets' based on music of the 16th century Scottish church. See also *All sons of Adam*, 1974 [J122], *Our Father whiche in Heaven art*, 1977 [J151] and *Si quis diliget me*, 1973 [J117]. The above recording is available for private study at the National Sound Archive.

NACH BERGAMO - ZUR HEIMAT　(1974)

Catalogue no.:　J124

Descriptive title:　　　　　　NACH BERGAMO - ZUR HEIMAT

Musical format:　　　　　　Sextet

Location of manuscript:　　S.A.C.

Analysis:　　*Moderato - andante - adagio - lento*

Performance length:

Composed:　1974　　　　**Revised:**

Instruments:　Flute, clarinet, percussion, piano, viola, cello

Publishing information:　　MS (1 p)

Recording details:

First performance:

　　　at:

　　　by:

Notes:　　　　15 bars of music marked 'To open the Fires of London Schoenberg Centenary Concert at the Queen Elizabeth Hall on September 19th '74. Done at Banertoon Rackwick, August 1974'.

First performance: March 9 1974

       at: The Town Hall, Adelaide, South Australia

       by: Mary Thomas, mezzo-soprano and the Fires of London, conducted by the composer

Notes: Commissioned by the Adelaide Festival of Arts. The text is by Randolph Stow. Miss Donnithorne was an Australian lady, possibly one of the models for Miss Havisham in Dickens' *Great Expectations*; jilted at the last minute, she became a recluse. A tape recording is available at the National Sound Archive for private study only.

ALL SONS OF ADAM (1974)

Catalogue no.: J122

Descriptive title: ALL SONS OF ADAM. Motet for ensemble. Anon. (Scottish 16th century) arranged Maxwell Davies.

Musical format: Septet

Location of manuscript: Boosey and Hawkes

Analysis: One continuous movement

Performance length: 6 minutes

Composed: 1974   **Revised:**

Instruments: Alto flute, clarinet in B flat, marimba, celesta, guitar, viola, cello

Publishing information: BOOSEY AND HAWKES. Full score (27pp) in the volume *Four Instrumental Motets*; full score and parts for hire.

Recording details: UNICORN-KANCHANA. Record, *Renaissance and Baroque Realisations* KP 8005; CD, UKCD 2044. The Fires of London, conducted by the composer.

First performance: February 20 1974

at: Queen Elizabeth Hall, London

by: The Fires of London, conducted by the composer

Notes: One of four 'instrumental motets' based on music of the 16th century Scottish church. See also *Si quis diliget me*, 1973 [J117], *Our Father whiche in Heaven art*, 1977 [J151] and *Psalm 124*, 1974 [J123]. The original is an anonymous hymn. A tape recording is available at the Naitonal Sound Archive for private study only.

DARK ANGELS (1974)

Catalogue no.:   J120

Descriptive title: DARK ANGELS for voice and guitar

Musical format: Mezzo-soprano and guitar

Location of manuscript: S.M.I.C. (MS and sketches)

Analysis: (i) The drowning brothers (ii) Dark angels (guitar solo) (iii) Dead fires

Performance length: 12 minutes

Composed: 1974   **Revised:**

Instruments: Mezzo-soprano, guitar

Publishing information: BOOSEY AND HAWKES.   Score (12pp) for sale.

Recording details: NONESUCH: Record, H 71342.   Jan DeGaetani, mezzo-soprano and Oscar Ghiglia, guitar.

First performance: July 31 1974

    at: Dartington Summer School

    by: Mary Thomas, mezzo-soprano and Timothy Walker, guitar

Notes: Text by George Mackay Brown from the poem-cycle *Fishermen with Ploughs*.   The above recording is available for private study at the National Sound Archive.

MISS DONNITHORNE'S MAGGOT   (1974)

Catalogue no.:   J121

Descriptive title: MISS DONNITHORNE'S MAGGOT. Music theatre work for soprano (or mezzo-soprano) and ensemble.

Musical format: Voice(s) and instruments

Location of manuscript:

Analysis: (i) Prelude (ii) Miss Donnithorne's Maggot (iii) Recitative (iv) Her Dump (v) Nocturne (instruments alone) (vi) Her Rant (vii) Recitative (viii) Her Reel

Performance length: 38 minutes

Composed: 1974   **Revised:**

Instruments: Flute (doubling piccolo and alto flute), clarinet in A, violin, cello, piano (doubling rubbed balloon and bosun's whistle), four mechanical metronomes to be operated by the flautist, clarinettist, violinist and cellist

Percussion (1 player): small and large suspended cymbals, bass drum and cymbal with foot pedal, large bass drum, side drum, large temple block, four wood blocks, tam-tam, football rattle, bell tree, sandpaper blocks, glass wind chimes, police and slide whistles, chamois leather rubbed on glass, balloon to pop, thunder sheet (or tam-tam), glockenspiel, marimba, crotales

Publishing information: BOOSEY AND HAWKES. Full score (68pp) for sale and hire; parts for hire.

Recording details: UNICORN-KANCHANA: CD, DKP (CD) 9052; Cassette, DKP (C) 9052. Mary Thomas, mezzo-soprano and the Fires of London, conducted by the composer.

continued ...

J.S. BACH: PRELUDE AND FUGUE IN C SHARP MAJOR (1974)

Catalogue no.: J125

Descriptive title: J.S. BACH: PRELUDE AND FUGUE IN C SHARP MAJOR, the '48', Book I. Realisation for ensemble.

Musical format: Sextet

Location of manuscript: Boosey and Hawkes

Analysis: Prelude: *Vivace* Fugue: *Allegro moderato*

Performance length: 5 minutes

Composed: 1974 **Revised:**

Instruments: Flute, clarinet in A (or basset clarinet in A), harpsichord, marimba, viola, cello

Publishing information: BOOSEY AND HAWKES. Full score (32pp) for sale in one volume with *Prelude and Fugue in C sharp minor*; full score and parts for hire.

Recording details: UNICORN-KANCHANA: Record, *Renaissance and Baroque Realisations* KP 8005; CD, UKCD 2044. The Fires of London, conducted by the composer.

First performance: November 27 1974

at: Queen Elizabeth Hall, London

by: The Fires of London

Notes: If played as a pair with the *Prelude and fugue in C sharp minor* [J113], that is to precede this piece. Originally conceived as an overture to the Schoenberg/Webern Chamber Symphony. A tape recording of a performance by The Fires of London is available at the National Sound Archive for private study only.

SONG FOR JENNY AND HER NEW BABY (1974)

Catalogue no.:   J126

Descriptive title: SONG FOR JENNY AND HER NEW BABY

Musical format: Unaccompanied SATB

Location of manuscript: S.M.I.C. (sketch)

Analysis: No tempo indicated

Performance length:

Composed: 1974   **Revised:**

Instruments: Soprano, Alto, Tenor and Bass

Publishing information: MS (1 p)

Recording details:

First performance:

    at:

    by:

Notes: Marked "SATB = Judith, Mary, Duncan, Alan".

BLACK FURROW, GRAY FURROW (1974)

Catalogue no.:   J127

Descriptive title: BLACK FURROW, GRAY FURROW

Musical format: Voice (treble clef), alto flute and marimba

Location of manuscript: S.M.I.C. (MS and sketch)

Analysis: *Adagio*

Performance length:

Composed: 1974   **Revised:**

Instruments: Voice (treble clef), alto flute, marimba

Publishing information: MS (2 pp)

Recording details:

First performance:

    at:

    by:

Notes: Text by George Mackay Brown. For James Murdoch.

WEDDING TELEGRAM   (?1974)

Catalogue no.:   J128

Descriptive title: WEDDING TELEGRAM FOR GARY
KETTEL

Musical format: Soprano, guitar and celesta

Location of manuscript: S.M.I.C. (MS)

Analysis: *Adagio - allegro - adagio - allegretto, adagio*

Performance length:

Composed: ?1974   **Revised:**

Instruments: Soprano, guitar, celesta

Publishing information: MS (2 pp)

Recording details:

First performance:

          at:

          by:

Notes: In a bag with other material dated 1974.

SKETCH 2   (?1974)

Catalogue no.:   J129

Descriptive title:	UNTITLED [Sketch 2]
Musical format:	Duet
Location of manuscript:	S.M.I.C.
Analysis: *Andante*	
Performance length:	
Composed: ?1974	**Revised:**
Instruments: Flute, bassoon	
Publishing information:	MS (1 p)
Recording details:	
First performance:	
at:	
by:	

Notes: Marked "For Judith and Roy". In a bag with other material dated 1974.

YESTERDAY   **(1974)**

Catalogue no.:   J130

Descriptive title: YESTERDAY: Lennon and McCartney,
                                 arranged Maxwell Davies

Musical format: Guitar solo

Location of manuscript: S.A.C.

Analysis:

Performance length:

Composed: 1974   **Revised:**

Instruments: Guitar

Publishing information: No publisher.   Printed by Southern
                                 Printing Service, Maidstone.

Recording details: OISEAU-LYRE: Record, DSLO 3.
                                 Timothy Walker, guitar.

First performance:

     at:

     by:

Notes: MS marked "For Tim Walker". The above recording is
                     available for private study at the National Sound
                     Archive.

AVE MARIS STELLA (1975)

Catalogue no.: J131

Descriptive title: AVE MARIS STELLA for unconducted ensemble

Musical format: Sextet

Location of manuscript: SMC (MS)

Analysis: (i) *Andante* (ii) *Poco a poco moto* (iii) *Allegro* (iv) *Prestissimo* (v) *Allegro* (vi) *Moderato, recitativo* (vii) *Presto* (viii) *Tempo d'inizio* (ix) *Lento molto*

Performance length: 32 minutes

Composed: 1975 **Revised:**

Instruments: Flute (doubling alto flute), clarinet in A (or basset clarinet in A), marimba (four octaves C to C), viola, cello, piano

Publishing information: BOOSEY AND HAWKES. Full score (46 pp) for sale and hire; parts for hire.

Recording details: UNICORN-KANCHANA: Record, KP 8002; CD, UKCD 2038. The Fires of London.

First performance: May 27 1975

at: The Bath Festival

by: The Fires of London

Notes: Commissioned by the Bath Festival 'In Memoriam Hans Juda'. Conceived as both a challenge and a tribute to the virtuosity of the Fires of London. See also [J184]. A record of a performance by The Fires of London, conducted by the composer, is available at the National Sound Archive for private study only.

DOOR OF THE SUN (1975)

Catalogue no.:   J132

Descriptive title: THE DOOR OF THE SUN for viola

Musical format: Viola solo

Location of manuscript: S.M.I.C. (MS)

Analysis: (i) *Allegro* (ii) *Lento* (iii) *Presto* (iv) *Lento* (v) *Moderato*

Performance length: 6 minutes

Composed: 1975   **Revised:**

Instruments: Viola

Publishing information: BOOSEY AND HAWKES. Score (4pp) for sale.

Recording details: CRI (Composer's Recordings Incorporated): Cassette, *Twentieth Century Viola Anthology, Vol. II* ACS 6017. John Graham, viola.

First performance: March 9 1976

at: A BBC Invitation Concert at the Great Hall of the University of Surrey

by: Duncan Druce, viola

Notes: The title is taken from a poem by George Mackay Brown. A tape recording of the first performance is available at the National Sound Archive for private study only.

KESTREL PACED ROUND THE SUN

(1975)

Catalogue no.:　J133

Descriptive title:　　　THE KESTREL PACED ROUND THE SUN for flute

Musical format:　　　Flute solo

Location of manuscript:　　S.M.I.C. (MS)

Analysis:　Three short movements

Performance length:　　4 minutes

Composed:　1975　　**Revised:**

Instruments:　Flute

Publishing information:　　BOOSEY AND HAWKES.　Score for sale in one volume with *Solita* (10 pp in toto).

Recording details:

First performance:　　　March 9 1976

　　　　at:　A BBC Invitation Concert at the Great Hall of the University of Surrey

　　　　by:　Judith Pearce, flute

Notes:　　　The title relates to a poem by George Mackay Brown. A tape recording of the first performance is available at the National Sound Archive for private study only. See also *Solita* [J82].

SEVEN BRIGHTNESSES   (1975)

Catalogue no.:   J134

Descriptive title: THE SEVEN BRIGHTNESSES for clarinet in B flat

Musical format: Clarinet solo

Location of manuscript: S.M.I.C. (MS)

Analysis: (i) *Presto* (ii) *Adagio* (iii) *Adagio expressivo* (iv) *Moderato* (v) *Allegro*

Performance length: 4 minutes

Composed: 1975   **Revised:**

Instruments: B flat clarinet

Publishing information: BOOSEY AND HAWKES.   Score (4pp) for sale.

Recording details:

First performance: October 12 1975

    at: William and Mary College, Williamsburg, Virginia

    by: Alan Hacker, clarinet

Notes: The title is taken from a poem by George Mackay Brown. A tape recording of a performance by Alan Hacker is available at the National Sound Archive for private study only.

THREE STUDIES FOR PERCUSSION

(1975)

Catalogue no.:   J135

Descriptive title: THREE STUDIES FOR PERCUSSION
for eleven percussionists

Musical format: Eleven percussion players

Location of manuscript: S.M.I.C. (sketch)

Analysis: (i) *Allegro* (ii) *Andante* (iii) *Presto*

Performance length: 5 minutes

Composed: 1975   **Revised:**

Instruments: Concert xylophone, soprano xylophone, alto xylophone, bass xylophone, soprano glockenspiel, alto glockenspiel, bass metallophone, deep bass metallophone, small wood block, small temple block, small suspended cymbal

Publishing information: CHESTER MUSIC. Full score (45 pp) and set of parts for sale.

Recording details:

First performance: October 15 1975

   at: Gosforth High School, Newcastle-upon-Tyne

   by: Gosforth School Percussion Ensemble, directed by Peter Swan.

Notes: Composed for Gosforth High School, Northumberland. The movements may be performed separately, or together as a three-movement work.

MY LADY LOTHIAN'S LILTE   (1975)

Catalogue no.:   J136

Descriptive title: MY LADY LOTHIAN'S LILTE for ensemble and mezzo-soprano obbligato (realisation)

Musical format: Voice(s) and instruments

Location of manuscript: S.M.I.C. (MS and sketch)

Analysis: One continuous movement - *Lento*

Performance length: 6 minutes

Composed: 1975   **Revised:**

Instruments: Mezzo-soprano, alto flute, bass clarinet, viola, cello Percussion (2 players): marimba, glockenspiel

Publishing information: BOOSEY AND HAWKES. Full score (24 pp) for sale in one volume with *Kinloche His Fantassie*; full score and parts for hire.

Recording details:

First performance: August 20 1975

at: Dartington Summer School

by: Mary Thomas (mezzo-soprano) and the Fires of London, conducted by the composer

Notes: The voice doubles the viola part except at the end when it is left lilting. See also *Kinloche His Fantassie* [J139].

STEVIE'S FERRY TO HOY   (1975)

Catalogue no.:   J137

Descriptive title: STEVIE'S FERRY TO HOY for piano
                                (elementary)

Musical format: Piano solo

Location of manuscript: S.M.I.C. (MS)

Analysis: (i) Calm water (ii) Choppy seas (iii) Safe landing

Performance length: 5 minutes

Composed: 1975   **Revised:**

Instruments: Piano

Publishing information: BOOSEY AND HAWKES. Score (3 pp)
                                for sale.

Recording details:

First performance:

      at:

      by:

Notes: Intended for Grade II pianists.

THREE ORGAN VOLUNTARIES   (1976)

Catalogue no.:   J138

Descriptive title:	THREE ORGAN VOLUNTARIES (formerly THREE PRELUDES FOR ORGAN)
Musical format:	Organ solo
Location of manuscript:	Archie Bevan, Artistic Director, St. Magnus Festival (photocopy with Gerard McBurney)

Analysis:

Performance length: 4 minutes

Composed: 1976   **Revised:**

Instruments: Organ

Publishing information: CHESTER MUSIC. Score (7 pp) for sale.

Recording details: PRO ARTE: Record, PRO PR 168. James Parsons, organ.

First performance: July 31 1979

at: Vestervig Kirke, Denmark

by: Jesper Jørgen Jensen, organ

Notes: Written for Mrs Elizabeth Bevan. Arrangements of 16th century Scottish church music: (i) *Psalm 124* (David Peebles) (ii) *O God abufe* (John Fethy) (iii) *All sons of Adam* (Anon.).

KINLOCHE HIS FANTASSIE (1976)

Catalogue no.: J139

Descriptive title: KINLOCHE HIS FANTASSIE. Realisation for ensemble.

Musical format: Sextet

Location of manuscript: S.M.I.C. (MS)

Analysis: One continuous movement - *Moderato*

Performance length: 4 minutes

Composed: 1976   **Revised:**

Instruments: Flute, clarinet, harpsichord, glockenspiel, violin, cello

Publishing information: BOOSEY AND HAWKES. Full score (24pp) for sale in one volume with *My Lady Lothian's Lilte*; full score and parts for hire.

Recording details: UNICORN-KANCHANA: Record, *Renaissance and Baroque Realisations* KP 8005; CD, UKCD 2044. The Fires of London, conducted by the composer. UNICORN-KANCHANA: *A Celebration of Scotland*; CD, DKP (CD) 9070, Cassette, DKP (C) 9070. Members of the Scottish Chamber Orchestra, conducted by the composer.

First performance: August 19 1976

at: Dartington Summer School

by: The Fires of London, conducted by the composer

Notes: Arrangement of a fantasy by the 16th century Scottish composer, William Kinloch. A tape recording of a performance by the Fires of London, conducted by the composer, is available at the National Sound Archive for private study only. See also My Lady Lothian's Lilte [J136].

ANAKREONTIKA (1976)

Catalogue no.:   J140

Descriptive title: ANAKREONTIKA. Greek songs for mezzo-soprano and ensemble.

Musical format: Voice(s) and instruments

Location of manuscript: S.M.I.C. (MS); Gerald McBurney (Sketches)

Analysis: Five songs combined with instrumental commentaries into a single movement

Performance length: 15 minutes

Composed: 1976   **Revised:**

Instruments: Mezzo-soprano, alto flute, harpsichord, cello
Percussion (1 player): glockenspiel, marimba, small and very small wood blocks, tambourine, crotales (C sharp, G and A)

Publishing information: CHESTER MUSIC. Full score (17 pp) and parts on sale separately.

Recording details:

First performance: September 17 1976

at: Queen Elizabeth Hall, London

by: Mary Thomas, mezzo-soprano and the Fires of London, conducted by the composer

Notes: The text is late ancient Greek in the style of Anakreon. The first drafts are marked "Anankreontics"

BLIND FIDDLER   (1976)

Catalogue no.:   J141

Descriptive title: THE BLIND FIDDLER. Song cycle for
                                   mezzo-soprano and ensemble.

Musical format: Voice(s) and instruments

Location of manuscript: S.M.I.C. (MS)

Analysis: Seven songs interspersed with seven dances

Performance length: 43 minutes

Composed: 1976   **Revised:**

Instruments: Mezzo-soprano, flute (doubling piccolo and alto flute),
clarinet in A or basset clarinet (doubling bass clarinet),
harpsichord (doubling celesta), guitar, violin, cello
Percussion (1 player): marimba, large and very small
wood blocks, small Chinese cymbal, large and small
temple block, spoons, maracas (or small shaker), tabor,
castanet machine, large and small suspended cymbals,
bell tree, bones, crotales, rototoms, two timpani, large
Japanese temple gong placed on pedal timpani, very
large nipple gong, B flat antique cymbal to be played by
singer

Publishing information: BOOSEY AND HAWKES. Full score (50
                                   pp) for sale and hire; parts for hire.

Recording details:

First performance: February 16 1976

              at: Freemason's Hall, Edinburgh

              by: Mary Thomas, mezzo-soprano and the Fires of London,
                         conducted by the composer

continued ...

Notes: Commissioned by the Newtown Concert Society, Edinburgh. The text is from *A Spell for Green Corn* by George Mackay Brown. A tape recording of a performance by Mary Thomas and The Fires of London, conducted by the composer, is available at the National Sound Archive for private study only.

The Fires of London at the 1981 St. Albans Festival.
Left to right: Jonathan Williams — cello, Rosemary Furniss — violin,
Stephen Pruslin — piano, David Campbell — clarinet, Philippa Davies — flute,
Gregory Knowles — percussion.

John Carewe

SYMPHONY NO. 1   (1976)

Catalogue no.:   J142

Descriptive title: SYMPHONY NO. 1

Musical format: Full orchestra

Location of manuscript:

Analysis: (i) *Presto* (ii) *Lento* (iii) *Adagio* (iv) *Presto*

Performance length: 53 minutes

Composed: 1976   **Revised:**

Instruments: Piccolo, two flutes (second doubling alto flute), two oboes, cor anglais, two clarinets, bass clarinet, two bassoons, contrabassoon, four horns, three trumpets, three trombones, timpani, harp, celesta, strings
Percussion (4 players): marimba, tubular bells, flexatone, glockenspiel, crotales

Publishing information: BOOSEY AND HAWKES. Pocket score (184 pp) for sale; full score and parts for hire.

Recording details: DECCA: HEAD 21. Philharmonia Orchestra, conducted by Simon Rattle.

First performance: February 20 1978

       at: Royal Festival Hall, London

       by: Philharmonia Orchestra, conducted by Simon Rattle

continued ...

Notes: Commissioned by the Philharmonia Orchestra. The composer has stated that he reached maturity as an orchestral composer in writing this first symphony, and the work builds on what he had learnt of orchestration and large design in the *Second Taverner Fantasia* and *Worldes Blis*. The orchestral colour, however, changes to 'Orkney music' as the sea is often heard in important parts for tuned percussion. A tape recording of the first performance is available at the National Sound Archive for private study only.

MARTYRDOM OF SAINT MAGNUS (1976)

Catalogue no.:   J143

Descriptive title:	THE MARTYRDOM OF SAINT MAGNUS. Chamber opera.
Musical format:	Chamber opera
Location of manuscript:	S.M.I.C. (Libretto); Mrs Judy Arnold (MS)

Analysis: One act of nine scenes without interval: (i) The Battle of Menai Strait (ii) The Temptations of Magnus (iii) The Curse of Blind Mary (iv) The Peace Parley (v) Magnus' Journey to the Isle of Egilsay (vi) Earl Hakon resolves to murder Magnus (vii) The Reporters (vii) The Sacrifice (ix) The Miracle

Performance length: 82 minutes

Composed: 1976   **Revised:**

Instruments: Mezzo-soprano, Tenor, two Baritones, Bass, flute (doubling piccolo and alto flute), clarinet in A (doubling bass clarinet), horn, two trumpets, guitar, viola, cello, double bass

Keyboards (1 player): harpsichord, celesta, keyboard carillon or Celtic harp (see Notes), slightly out-of-tune upright piano

Percussion (1 player): large and very large bass drums, pedal timpani, side drum, small snare drum, rototoms, large bowed cymbal, two Chinese cymbals, crotales, Burmese nipple gongs, tam-tam, very large Japanese gong, sandpaper blocks, blackboard, plastic soap dish, glockenspiel, marimba

Percussion to be played by singers, keyboard player and guitarist: four pairs of claves, flexatone, railway whistle, tabor, Australian Aboriginal bullroarer (optional)

continued ...

Publishing information:	BOOSEY AND HAWKES. Full score (170 pp) and study score for sale and hire; pocket score and libretto for sale; parts and vocal score for hire.
Recording details:	UNICORN-KANCHANA: CD, DKP (CD) 9100. The Music Theatre of Wales and the Scottish Chamber Orchestra, conducted by Michael Rafferty.
First performance:	June 18 1977
at:	The first St. Magnus Festival in Orkney
by:	Mary Thomas, mezzo-soprano, Neil Mackie, tenor, Michael Rippon and Brian Rayner Cook, baritone, Ian Comboy, bass and the Fires of London, conducted by the composer
Notes:	Commissioned by the BBC for the Silver Jubilee of Queen Elizabeth II. Libretto by the composer from the novel *Magnus* by George Mackay Brown. Magnus was a 12th century Earl of Orkney who was murdered by his cousin and soon became worshipped as a martyr.

If Celtic harp and keyboard carillon are not available, the part should be divided between harpsichord and celesta.

An arrangement of tenor arias was made in 1981 and first performed on June 23 1981 at the St. Magnus Festival by Neil Mackie, tenor, and Richard Hughes, organ. The score is available from Boosey and Hawkes. A tape recording of a performance by the artists of the first performance is available at the National Sound Archive for private study only.

PIANO PIECE (?1976)

Catalogue no.:　J144

Descriptive title: UNTITLED [Piano Piece]

Musical format: Piano solo (not indicated)

Location of manuscript: S.M.I.C. (sketch)

Analysis: No tempo indicated

Performance length:

Composed: ?1976　　**Revised:**

Instruments: Piano

Publishing information: MS (1 p)

Recording details:

First performance:

    at:

    by:

Notes: In a bag with other material dated 1976.

SILVER JUBILEE SALUTE   (1977)

Catalogue no.:   J145

Descriptive title:	The Orkney Strathspey and Reel Society's Silver Jubilee Salute to H.M. the Queen and the Duke of Edinburgh. W.R. Aim, arranged Maxwell Davies.
Musical format:	Septet
Location of manuscript:	S.A.C. (Sketch); S.M.I.C. (MS)

Analysis:

Performance length:

Composed: 1977   **Revised:**

Instruments: Flute (doubling piccolo), clarinet, horn, violin, cello, piano (doubling optional celesta)
Percussion (1 player): hi-hat cymbal, side drum with snares, bass drum with foot pedal

Publishing information: MS (4 pp)

Recording details:

First performance:

> **at:**

> **by:**

Notes: Arranged for the Fires of London for the 1979 St. Magnus Festival.

WESTERLINGS   (1977)

Catalogue no.:   J146

Descriptive title:	WESTERLINGS for SATB chorus
Musical format:	Unaccompanied chorus
Location of manuscript:	S.M.I.C. (MS and sketch)

Analysis: (i) Seascape (ii) First song: *A Golden Whale* (iii) Seascape II (iv) Second Song: *The Ancient Tryst* (v) Seascape III (vi) Third Song: *Our Gods Uncaring* (vii) Seascape IV (viii) Fourth Song: *Landfall* (ix) Prayer: *Orkney Norn*

Performance length:	15 minutes
Composed: 1977	**Revised:**
Instruments:	Soprano, Alto, Tenor and Bass
Publishing information:	BOOSEY AND HAWKES. Score (36pp) for sale and hire.

Recording details:

First performance: *Incomplete*: May 25 1977
Complete: October 15 1977

at: *Incomplete*: Uppsala University
Complete: BBC Concert Hall, Broadcasting House, London

by: *Incomplete*: Uppsala University Chamber Choir
Complete: The BBC Singers, conducted by John Aldis

Notes: Commissioned by Uppsala University for its quincentenary. The text is by George Mackay Brown. The first complete performance was broadcast on BBC Radio 3 on April 9 1987, and a tape recording of this is available at the National Sound Archive for private study only.

NORN PATER NOSTER   (1977)

Catalogue no.:   J147

Descriptive title: NORN PATER NOSTER.   Prayer for
                                    SATB chorus and organ.

Musical format: Chorus and organ

Location of manuscript: S.M.I.C. (MS)

Analysis: One continuous movement

Performance length: 3 minutes

Composed: 1977   **Revised:**

Instruments: Soprano, Alto, Tenor and Bass chorus, organ

Publishing information: BOOSEY AND HAWKES.   Score (8 pp)
                                     for sale.

Recording details:

First performance:

          at:

          by:

Notes: This is an adaptation by the composer of the last
                    section of *Westerlings* [J146].

RUNES FROM A HOLY ISLAND   (1977)

Catalogue no.:   J148

Descriptive title: RUNES FROM A HOLY ISLAND for
                                 ensemble

Musical format: Sextet

Location of manuscript: S.M.I.C. (MS and sketch)

Analysis: (i)*Andante* (ii) *Presto* (iii) *Andante moderato* (iv) *Lento*
                     (v) *Presto*

Performance length: 10 minutes

Composed: 1977   **Revised:**

Instruments: Alto flute, clarinet in A, viola, cello, celesta
                     Percussion (1 player): glockenspiel, four wood
                     blocks, Chinese cymbal, castanets, four-octave
                     marimba, bass drum

Publishing information: CHESTER MUSIC. Full score (17 pp)
                                 for sale and hire; parts for hire.

Recording details: UNICORN-KANCHANA: CD, UK CD
                                 2038; Cassette, DKP (C) 9033; Record,
                                 DKP 9033. The Fires of London,
                                 conducted by the composer.

First performance: *Broadcast*: November 6 1977
                                 Public: September 6 1978

     at: *Broadcast*: BBC Radio 4
                Public: Edinburgh International Festival

     by: The Fires of London, conducted by the composer

Notes: Commissioned by the BBC for the Radio 4 programme
                     Not Now, I'm Listening. The five 'runes' form a miniature
                     symphony with virtuoso marimba parts in the third and
                     fifth movements. A recording of a performance by the
                     Fires of London is available at the National Sound Archive
                     for private study only.

MIRROR OF WHITENING LIGHT   (1977)

Catalogue no.:   J149

Descriptive title: A MIRROR OF WHITENING LIGHT for ensemble

Musical format: 14 instrumentalists

Location of manuscript: S.M.I.C. (MS)

Analysis: One continuous movement

Performance length: 22 minutes

Composed: 1977   **Revised:**

Instruments: Flute (doubling piccolo), oboe (doubling cor anglais), clarinet in A, bassoon, horn, trumpet, trombone, celesta, violin I, violin II, viola, cello, double bass
Percussion (1 player): crotales, glockenspiel, marimba

Publishing information: BOOSEY AND HAWKES.   Full score (104 pp) and study score for sale and hire; parts for hire.

Recording details:

First performance: March 23 1977

          at: Queen Elizabeth Hall, London

          by: The London Sinfonietta, conducted by the composer

Notes: Commissioned by the London Sinfonietta with funds provided by the Arts Council of Great Britain.   The Mirror is the Pentland Firth as seen from Davies' Orkney home, but the title alludes to the process of alchemical transformation: *Speculum luminis dealbensis* - the 'whitening' process of turning base metal into gold.   A tape recording of a performance by the London Sinfonietta, conducted by Elgar Howarth, is available at the National Sound Archive for private study only.

AVE REX ANGELORUM (1977)

Catalogue no.: J150

Descriptive title: AVE REX ANGELORUM for SATB chorus with optional organ

Musical format: Unaccompanied chorus

Location of manuscript:

Analysis:

Performance length: 2 minutes

Composed: 1977 Revised:

Instruments: Soprano, Alto, Tenor and Bass chorus; optional organ

Publishing information: BOOSEY AND HAWKES. Score (4 pp) for sale.

Recording details:

First performance: December 18 1977

at: St. Magnus' Cathedral, Kirkwall, Orkney

by: Pupils of Kirkwall Grammar School, conducted by Norman Mitchell.

Notes: Written for Norman Mitchell and the choir of Kirkwall Grammar School. A tape recording is available at the National Sound Archive for private study only.

OUR FATHER WHICHE IN HEAVEN ART (1977)

Catalogue no.:   J151

Descriptive title: OUR FATHER WHICHE IN HEAVEN ART. Motet for ensemble. John Angus, arranged Maxwell Davies.

Musical format: Sextet

Location of manuscript: S.M.I.C. (MS)

Analysis: *Andante*

Performance length: 5 minutes

Composed: 1977   **Revised:**

Instruments: Flute, clarinet in B flat (doubling clarinet in E flat ad lib.), celesta, marimba, violin, cello

Publishing information: BOOSEY AND HAWKES. Full score for sale in the volume *Four Instrumental Motets* (27 pp); full score and parts for hire.

Recording details: UNICORN-KANCHANA: Record, *Renaissance and Baroque Realisations* KP 8005; CD, UK CD 2044. The Fires of London, conducted by the composer.

First performance: August 18 1977

at: Dartington Summer School

by: The Fires of London, conducted by the composer

Notes: One of four 'instrumental motets' derived from 16th century Scottish church music (see also *Si quis diliget me* [J117], *All sons of Adam* [J122] and *Psalm 124* [J123]). A tape recording is available at the National Sound Archive for private study only.

CANTATA PROFUNDA, Op. 2002   (1977)

Catalogue no.:   J152

Descriptive title: CANTATA PROFUNDA, Op. 2002

Musical format: Sextet ((i) and (iv)) and septet ((ii) and (iii))

Location of manuscript: Ian Kellam (MS)

Analysis: (i) *Adagio lamentoso* (ii) *Allegro*

Performance length: 40 seconds

Composed: 1977   **Revised:**

Instruments: "Heldentenor und übergrosses Hammercembalo"

Publishing information: MS (1 p)

Recording details:

First performance:

          at:

          by:

Notes: Signed "Meant as a LAMENT in the GRIPES at missing the Q.E.H. performance of Ian's work, Saturday 18th December 1977".

See also *Pussycat* [J100], which sets the same words in a similar fashion.

TWO FIDDLERS   (1978)

Catalogue no.:   J153

Descriptive title: THE TWO FIDDLERS. Opera in two
                                acts for children to perform.

Musical format: Opera

Location of manuscript: Boosey and Hawkes (Sketches);
                                photocopy of first draft with Gerard
                                McBurney

Analysis: 2 acts; characters: Storm Kolson (tenor), Gavin
                   (baritone), King of the Trolls (baritone), Queen of the
                   Trolls (soprano), Minister (bass) with Chorus of Trolls
                   and Chorus of Party Guests

Performance length: 55 minutes

Composed: 1978   **Revised:**

Instruments: Two flutes, oboe, two clarinets, bassoon, horn, two
                   trumpets, trombone, timpani, piano (doubling
                   metronome), solo string quintet (two violins, viola,
                   cello, double bass) or small string orchestra,
                   bagpipes (optional)
                   Percussion (6 players): two glockenspiels, marimba,
                   xylophone, four temple blocks, two wood blocks, two
                   brandy glasses (F and A flat), side drum, bass drum,
                   tam-tam, four suspended cymbals, pair of cymbals,
                   choke cymbal, tambourine, flexatone, referee's and
                   swannee whistles, football rattle, güiro, nightingale,
                   beaters and scrapers including a pair of knitting
                   needles, violin bows, plastic soap dish and brushes

continued ...

Publishing information:	BOOSEY AND HAWKES. Vocal score (81 pp) (including German translation) and choral score for sale and hire; libretto for sale; full score and parts for hire.

Recording details:

First performance:	June 16 1987
at:	St. Magnus Festival, Kirkwall, Orkney
by:	Pupils of the Kirkwall Grammar School, conducted by Norman Mitchell; produced by Jack Ridgeway.
Notes:	Libretto by the composer from a story by George Mackay Brown. Any of the male soloists' parts may be sung an octave higher by unchanged boys' voices or by girls' voices. Storm and Gavin both play solo violin on stage or else mime this while the two violins are played either off stage or in the orchestra. Devised for a slightly older age range than *Cinderella*, perhaps for children from 10 to 14, but the orchestral instruments are intended to be played by non-specialist schoolchildren. See also [J154]. A tape recording of a performance by the artists of the first performance is available at the National Sound Archive for private study only.

DANCES FROM 'THE TWO FIDDLERS' (1978)

Catalogue no.:   J154

Descriptive title: DANCES FROM 'THE TWO FIDDLERS' for ensemble

Musical format: Sextet

Location of manuscript: S.M.I.C. (MS)

Analysis: One continuous movement

Performance length: 7 minutes

Composed: 1978   **Revised:**

Instruments: Piccolo, bass clarinet, violin, cello, piano
Percussion (1 player): four temple blocks, small and large wood blocks, bass drum with foot pedal, side drum with snares, maracas

Publishing information: BOOSEY AND HAWKES. Full score (9 pp) for sale and hire; parts for hire.

Recording details: UNICORN-KANCHANA: *A Celebration of Scotland* CD, DKP (CD) 9070; Cassette, DKP (C) 9070. Members of the Scottish Chamber Orchestra, conducted by the composer.

First performance: October 6 1978

at: Queen Elizabeth Hall, London

by: The Fires of London

Notes: Adaptation of Orkney fiddle tunes. Dances in different keys and tempi are spliced together to make a single movement, led by the violinist, who should stand. See *The Two Fiddlers* [J153] and also *Dances From 'The Two Fiddlers'* [J220].

JONGLEUR DE NOTRE DAME (1978)

Catalogue no.: J155

Descriptive title: LE JONGLEUR DE NOTRE DAME. Masque for baritone, mime/juggler, ensemble and children's band.

Musical format: Voice(s) and instruments

Location of manuscript: S.M.I.C.

Analysis: Masque

Performance length: 50 minutes

Composed: 1978 **Revised:**

Instruments: Flute (doubling piccolo and alto flute), clarinet in A (doubling bass clarinet), violin, cello, piano (doubling celesta)
Percussion: marimba, glockenspiel, tambourine, maracas, sanctus bells
Children's band: Three flutes, oboe, two clarinets, three trumpets, tambourine, side drum, bass drum

Publishing information: CHESTER MUSIC. Full score (66 pp) for sale and hire; instrumental and children's band parts for hire.

Recording details:

First performance: June 18 1978

at: Stromness at the St. Magnus Festival, Orkney

by: Mark Furneaux, mime/juggler, Michael Rippon, baritone and the Fires of London, conducted by the composer, and the Stromness Academy Wind Band, conducted by Jean Leonard.

continued ...

Notes: Commissioned by the Royal Bank of Scotland. Text by the composer based on a mediaeval French legend. The flautist, clarinettist and percussionist are costumed as monks and carry out simple pantomime acting parts, necessitating that their music be played from memory. The violinist is costumed as the Virgin Mary and remains visibly seated on an altar throughout the performance.

SALOME   (1978)

Catalogue no.:   J156

Descriptive title:	SALOME
Musical format:	Ballet
Location of manuscript:	S.M.I.C. (MS and sketch)

Analysis: Nine scenes in two acts. Act I: (i) The Roman Occupation (ii) The Struggle for Power (iii) The Escape of John the Baptist (iv) The Baptism (v) The Imprisonment of John the Baptist

Act II: (i) Herod's Dark Night of the Soul (ii) The Triumph of Herod (iii) Herod's Feast (iv) Execution and Apotheosis of John the Baptist

Performance length: 120 minutes

Composed: 1978   **Revised:**

Instruments: Two flutes (second doubling piccolo and alto flute), two oboes, two clarinets (second doubling bass clarinet), two bassoons (second doubling double bassoon), four horns, two trumpets, two trombones, timpani, harp, celesta, strings

Percussion (5 players): *I* - bass drum, very large bass drum, foot bass drum, tambourine, rototoms, small and large wood blocks, tam-tam, small Chinese cymbal, cymbal, very deep nipple gong, anvil, tabor, tubular bells

II - small and large wood blocks, small and large temple blocks, glockenspiel, flexatone, small, bowed suspended cymbal, tam-tam, crotales, bell tree, slapstick, blackboard played with fingernails

III - small Chinese cymbal, medium, bowed suspended cymbal, crotales, tenor drum, glockenspiel, small and large scaffolding pipes, rototoms, small and large wood blocks, small and large temple blocks, maracas

continued ...

page 182

IV - small, medium and large suspended cymbals, large, bowed suspended cymbal, tubular bells, tam-tam, tom-tom, anvil, maracas, tambourine
V - marimba, large North African metal castanets

For reduced orchestra: two flutes (second doubling piccolo and alto flute), two oboes (second doubling cor anglais), two clarinets (second doubling bass clarinet), two bassoons, two horns, two trumpets, two trombones, timpani, celesta, harp, strings - first violins (min. 5), second violins (min. 4), violas (min. 3), cellos (min. 3), double basses (min. 2)

Percussion (3 players): *I* - glockenspiel, medium, bowed cymbal, flexatone, suspended scaffolding pipes, tam-tam, tambourine, rototoms, two wood blocks, two temple blocks

II - crotales, marimba, small, bowed cymbal, three suspended cymbals, deep nipple gong, tam-tam, tenor drum, very large bass drum

III - crotales, tubular bells, small Chinese cymbal, two suspended cymbals, large, bowed cymbal, bell tree, anvil, two wood blocks, maracas, very large bass drum

Publishing information:	BOOSEY AND HAWKES. Pocket score for sale; full score (299 pp) and parts (both versions) for hire.
Recording details:	EMI: 3 Records, 157-39270/1/2

continued ...

First performance: November 10th 1978

    at: Circus Building, Copenhagen

    by: Danish Radio Orchestra, conducted by Janos Fürst. Choreography by Flemming Flindt.

Notes: Commissioned by Flemming Flindt to launch his new Flemming Flindt Circus Company. Each of the two acts may be performed separately in concert. A concert suite drawn from both acts is suggested in the full score, and was first performed in this form on March 16 1979 at the Royal Festival Hall, London, by the London Symphony Orchestra conducted by David Atherton. A reduction for theatre orchestra was commissioned by the Dallas Ballet, Texas in 1982. Full score and parts for these suites are for hire from Boosey and Hawkes. The above recording is available at the National Sound Archive for private study only.

FOUR LESSONS   (1978)

Catalogue no.:   J157

Descriptive title: FOUR LESSONS for two clavichords

Musical format: Two clavichords (or keyboards; see Notes)

Location of manuscript: Mrs Sylvia Junge

Analysis: (i) *Lento* (ii) *Moderato* (iii) *Allegro* (iv) *Adagio*

Performance length: 10 minutes

Composed: 1978   **Revised:**

Instruments: Two clavichords

Publishing information: BOOSEY AND HAWKES. Performing score (11 pp) for sale.

Recording details:

First performance: August 23 1978

    at: Dartington Summer School

    by: Bernard Roberts and Sylvia Junge, clavichords

Notes: These pieces can also be played on "two keyboard instruments of any kind, alike or contrasting" according to the composer, so long as they create a reasonable balance of sound.

BLACK PENTECOST   (1979)

Catalogue no.:   **J158**

Descriptive title: BLACK   PENTECOST   for
mezzo-soprano, baritone and orchestra

Musical format: Voice(s) and orchestra

Location of manuscript: S.M.I.C. (MS and sketch)

Analysis: (i) *Adagio* (ii) *Lentissimo* (iii) *Lentissimo - allegro* (iv) *Andante*

Performance length: 45 minutes

Composed: 1979   **Revised:**

Instruments: Mezzo-soprano, Baritone and orchestra of two flutes, alto flute, two oboes, cor anglais, two clarinets, bass clarinet, two bassoons, contrabassoon, four horns, three trumpets, two trombones, timpani, celesta, strings
Percussion (5 players): marimba, very large bass drum, glockenspiel, crotales, small suspended Chinese cymbal, pair of maracas, slapstick, very high and piercing claves, small resonant metal bowl on kettle-drum, rototoms, two flexatones, tam-tam (with plastic soap dish)

Publishing information: CHESTER MUSIC. Full score (166 pp) for sale and hire; parts for hire.

Recording details:

First performance: May 11 1982

     at: Royal Festival Hall, London

     by: Philharmonia Orchestra, conducted by Simon Rattle. Jan DeGaetani (mezzo-soprano) and Michael Rippon (baritone).

Notes: Commissioned by the Philharmonia Orchestra. Text drawn from the novel *Greenvoe* by George Mackay Brown. A tape recording is available at the National Sound Archive for private study only.

SOLSTICE OF LIGHT   (1979)

Catalogue no.:   J159

Descriptive title: SOLSTICE OF LIGHT for tenor, SATB
                                  chorus and organ

Musical format: Tenor, chorus and organ

Location of manuscript: S.M.I.C. (MS and sketch)

Analysis: (i) New Hills and Lochs and Shores (ii) The Mild Circle of
                     the Sun (iii) We Rowed Blindly North and North (iv) Green
                     Whirls of Melted Ice (v) The Hills, the Skies, the Sweet and
                     the Salt Waters (vi) Earthbreakers, Hewers of Mighty
                     Stone (vii) Circles of Stone on the Blank Moor (viii)
                     Solstice of Light (ix) The Celtic Priests (x) The White
                     Weave of Peace (xi) Hawkship (xii) Norsemen (xiii)
                     Invocation of the Dove (xiv) Prayer for These Islands:
                     New Troves. (Performed continuously)

Performance length: 45 minutes

Composed: 1979   **Revised:**

Instruments: Tenor solo, Soprano, Alto, Tenor and Bass chorus
                   and organ

Publishing information: BOOSEY AND HAWKES. Full score
                                  (75 pp) for sale and hire.

Recording details:

First performance: June 18 1979

       at: St. Magnus Festival, Orkney

       by: Neil Mackie, tenor, Richard Hughes, organ and the
                 St. Magnus Singers, conducted by Norman Mitchell

Notes: Text by George Mackay Brown. A tape recording of
                 the first performance is available at the National
                 Sound Archive for private study only.

NOCTURNE   (1979)

Catalogue no.:   J160

Descriptive title: NOCTURNE for alto flute

Musical format: Alto flute solo

Location of manuscript: Philippa Davies

Analysis: One continuous movement

Performance length: 5 minutes

Composed: 1979   **Revised:**

Instruments: Alto flute

Publishing information: BOOSEY AND HAWKES. Score (4 pp) for sale.

Recording details:

First performance: January 28 1983

at: Wigmore Hall, London

by: Philippa Davies, alto flute

Notes: The dedication reads "For Philippa".

KIRKWALL SHOPPING SONGS   (1979)

Catalogue no.:   J161

Descriptive title: KIRKWALL SHOPPING SONGS for young children to sing and play

Musical format: Children's voices and instruments

Location of manuscript: S.M.I.C. (MS and sketch)

Analysis: (i) Song: When I got out of bed, my mother said to me (ii) Song: When you go down our street (iii) Instrumental interlude: The big tree (iv) Song: I must buy fat pig's fry (v) Instrumental interlude: At the Bakery (vi) Song: Oh Mr Spence, I've only got Ten Pence (vii) Instrumental interlude: Hoy Sound (vii) Song: Down that stair there's a lady fair (ix) Song: It must be time to go home to tea

Performance length: 20 minutes

Composed: 1979   **Revised:**

Instruments: Treble voices, recorders, percussion, piano

Publishing information: BOOSEY AND HAWKES. Performing set (Teacher's score, four tuned and two untuned percussion parts) (78 pp) on sale; Choral score for voices and recorders on sale in packets of ten.

Recording details:

First performance: June 16 1977

      at: St. Magnus Festival, Orkney

      by: Pupils of the Papdale Primary School, conducted by Glenys Hughes

Notes: Text by the composer. The intended age of the performers is 6 to 10. The six songs are in unison. A tape recording is available at the National Sound Archive for private study only.

LIGHTHOUSE   (1979)

Catalogue no.:   J162

Descriptive title:	THE LIGHTHOUSE. Chamber opera in one act.
Musical format:	Chamber opera
Location of manuscript:	S.M.I.C. (MS)

Analysis: One act with prologue. Prologue: *The Court of Enquiry* Act I: *The Cry of the Beast*

Performance length:	75 minutes
Composed: 1979	**Revised:**

Instruments: Tenor (Officer 1, Sandy), Baritone (Officer 2, Blazes), Bass (Officer 3, Arthur and Voice of the Cards), flute (doubling piccolo and alto flute), clarinet in A (doubling bass clarinet), horn, trumpet in C, trombone, piano (doubling celesta, slightly out-of-tune upright piano, flexatone and referee's whistle), guitar (doubling banjo and bass drum), violin (doubling tam-tam), viola (doubling flexatone), cello, double bass
Percussion (1 player): marimba, four timpani, glockenspiel, bass drum, pair of maracas, rototom, small suspended cymbal, bones, tambourine, tom-toms, snare drum, two octaves of crotales

Publishing information: CHESTER MUSIC. Miniature score and libretto for sale; vocal score (137 pp) for sale and hire; full score and parts for hire.

Recording details:

continued ...

First performance: September 2 1980

      at: Edinburgh International Festival

      by: Neil Mackie, tenor, Michael Rippon, baritone, David Wilson-Johnson, bass and the Fires of London, conducted by Richard Dufallo. Directed by David William.

Notes: Commissioned by the Edinburgh International Festival. Winner of the first Tennent Caledonian Award. Libretto by the composer, based on a true incident of 1900 when three lighthouse keepers disappeared from the Flannan Isles lighthouse, described by Craig Mair in his book on the Stevenson family of Edinburgh, lighthouse engineers. A tape recording is available at the National Sound Archive for private study only.

A QUIET MEMORY OF BOB JENNINGS

(1979)

Catalogue no.:   J163

Descriptive title: A QUIET MEMORY OF BOB JENNINGS

Musical format: String trio

Location of manuscript: S.M.I.C. (MS)

Analysis: *Adagio molto*

Performance length:

Composed: 1979   **Revised:**

Instruments: Violin, viola, cello

Publishing information: MS (1 p)

Recording details:

First performance:

      at:

      by:

Notes: MS marked "For Margaret Jennings".

CINDERELLA   (1980)

Catalogue no.:   J164

Descriptive title: CINDERELLA. Pantomime opera in two
                                 acts for young children to play and sing.

Musical format: Pantomime opera

Location of manuscript: S.M.I.C. (MS and sketch)

Analysis: Two acts

Performance length: 50 minutes

Composed: 1980   **Revised:**

Instruments: Descant recorder, treble recorder, tenor recorder (soli,
                   but multiple recorders can be used in some loud
                   sections), trumpet in B flat, piano, solo strings — two
                   violins, viola (optional), cello, double bass — or small
                   string orchestra (including viola)
                   Percussion (6 players): *I* - soprano glockenspiel, alto
                   xylophone, flexatone
                   II - alto glockenspiel, tenor xylophone, railway whistle,
                   balloon
                   III - bass xylophone, chime bars, two bongos, four temple
                   blocks, tambourine, bosun's whistle
                   IV - side drum, balloon, maracas, castanets, tambourine
                   V - suspended cymbal, clashed cymbals, two wood
                   blocks, duck call, sandpaper, sleighbells, triangle
                   VI - bass drum, referee's and swannee whistles, tam-tam,
                   dijeridu or equivalent

Publishing information: CHESTER MUSIC. Vocal score (71 pp),
                                 parts and libretto for sale; full score for
                                 sale and hire.

Recording details:

continued ...

First performance: June 21 1980

at: St. Magnus Festival, Krikwall, Orkney

by: Pupils of Papdale Primary School and Kirkwall Grammar School, conducted by Glenys Hughes. Produced by Marlene Mainland.

Notes: Libretto by the composer. Suitable for children between the ages of 8 and 12, although the Ugly Sisters can be sung an octave lower by boys with broken voices. The pianist must be quite advanced and some suggestions are indicated for modifying hard stretches for young players wih small hands. It is suggested that producers amend local Orkney references to their own areas. A tape recording is available at the National Sound Archive for private study only.

YELLOW CAKE REVUE   (1980)

Catalogue no.:   J165

Descriptive title: THE YELLOW CAKE REVUE.
Anti-nuclear cabaret for singer/reciter
and piano.

Musical format: Voice(s) and piano

Location of manuscript: S.M.I.C. (MS)

Analysis: (i) Tourist Board Song: O come to sunny Warbeth (ii)
Patriotic Song: You've heard of the man with the
pacemaker (iii) Piano interlude: Farewell to
Stromness (iv) Recitation - Nuclear Job Interview 1:
The Security Guard (v) Uranium's Daughter's Dance:
They said, when they'd extracted the uranium from
the ore (vi) Recitation - Nuclear Job Interview 2: The
Truck Driver (vii) Atlantic Breezes (viii) Recitation -
Nuclear Job Interview 3: The Mental Health Worker
(ix) Piano Interlude: Yesnaby Ground (x) The Terrorist
Song: Have you heard of the terrorist suicide squad?
(xi) The Triumph of the Cockroach: As earthquakes
subsided

Performance length: 25 minutes

Composed: 1980   **Revised:**

Instruments: Singer/reciter and piano

Publishing information: BOOSEY AND HAWKES. Full score
(36 pp) for sale.

Recording details:

continued ...

First performance: June 21 1980

at: St. Magnus Festival, Kirkwall, Orkney

by: Eleanor Bron, reciter and the composer, piano.

Notes: Text by the composer, as a contribution to the campaign to stop the Orkney Islands becoming a site for uranium mining, 'yellow cake' being uranium ore. The songs are tonal and may be transposed to suit male or female voices. See also *Farewell to Stromness* [J166] and *Yesnaby Ground* [J167].

FAREWELL TO STROMNESS (1980)

Catalogue no.: J166

Descriptive title: FAREWELL TO STROMNESS. Piano interlude from *The Yellow Cake Revue*.

Musical format: Piano solo

Location of manuscript:

Analysis: At a slow walking pace

Performance length: 5 minutes

Composed: 1980   **Revised:**

Instruments: Piano

Publishing information: BOOSEY AND HAWKES. Score for sale in one volume with *Yesnaby Ground* (5 pp in toto)

Recording details: UNICORN-KANCHANA: *A Celebration of Scotland* CD, DKP (CD) 9070; Cassette, DKP (C) 9070. The composer, piano.
MUSICA NOVA: CD in preparation. Richard Deering, piano.

First performance: June 21st 1980

    at: St. Magnus Festival, Kirkwall, Orkney

    by: The composer, piano

Notes: Originally one of the interludes from *The Yellow Cake Revue* [J165]. For pianists of Grade IV standard. A solo guitar version [J171] is also available and is on sale from Boosey and Hawkes.

YESNABY GROUND   (1980)

Catalogue no.:   J167

Descriptive title: YESNABY GROUND. Piano interlude
                                from *The Yellow Cake Revue*.

Musical format: Piano solo

Location of manuscript:

Analysis: At a fast walking pace

Performance length: 2 minutes

Composed: 1980   **Revised:**

Instruments: Piano

Publishing information: BOOSEY AND HAWKES. Score for
                                sale in one volume with *Farewell to
                                Stromness* (5 pp in toto).

Recording details: UNICORN-KANCHANA: *A
                                Celebration of Scotland* CD, DKP
                                (CD) 9070; Cassette, DKP (C) 9070.
                                The composer, piano.

First performance: June 21 1980

       at: St. Magnus Festival, Kirkwall, Orkney

       by: The composer, piano

Notes: Originally one of the interludes from *The Yellow Cake
                  Revue* [J165]. Yesnaby is famous for its great cliffs.
                  For pianists of Grade IV standard.

WELCOME TO ORKNEY   (1980)

Catalogue no.:   J168

Descriptive title: A WELCOME TO ORKNEY for
                            ensemble

Musical format: 14 instrumentalists

Location of manuscript: S.M.I.C. (MS)

Analysis: One continuous movement: *Allegro*

Performance length: 7 minutes

Composed: 1980   Revised:

Instruments: Flute, oboe, clarinet in A, bassoon, horn, two string
                 quartets, double bass

Publishing information: BOOSEY AND HAWKES. Full score
                                 (25 pp) and set of parts for sale and
                                 hire.

Recording details:

First performance: June 20 1980

          at: St. Magnus Festival, Kirkwall, Orkney

          by: Pupils of Chetham's School of Music, Manchester

Notes: Written for pupils of Chetham's School of Music to
               play as an overture at the St. Magnus Festival. A tape
               recording is available at the National Sound Archive
               for private study only.

LITTLE QUARTET No. 1   (1980)

Catalogue no.:   J169

Descriptive title: LITTLE QUARTET No. 1 for string quartet

Musical format: String quartet (young musicians)

Location of manuscript: S.M.I.C. (Sketches)

Analysis: Slow - very fast - slow (played without a break) (see Notes)

Performance length: 8 minutes

Composed: 1980   **Revised:**

Instruments: String quartet

Publishing information: BOOSEY AND HAWKES. Full score for sale in one volume with *Little Quartet No. 2* (20 pp in toto) and hire; parts for hire.

Recording details:

First performance: July 26 1982

     at: Dartington Summer School

     by: The Medici String Quartet

Notes: A tape recording is available at the National Sound Archive for private study only. The manuscript is marked *"Andante - allegro - lento"*. See also *Little Quartet No. 2* [J177]

SYMPHONY NO. 2   (1980)

Catalogue no.:   J170

Descriptive title: SYMPHONY NO. 2

Musical format: Full orchestra

Location of manuscript: S.M.I.C. (MS and sketch)

Analysis: (i) *Allegro molto* (ii) *Adagio* (iii) *Allegro molto* (iv) *Adagio - allegro*

Performance length: 50 minutes

Composed: 1980   **Revised:**

Instruments: Piccolo (doubling alto flute), two flutes, two oboes, two clarinets in A, bass clarinet, two bassoons, contrabassoon, four horns, three trumpets, two trombones, timpani, harp and strings

Percussion (3 players): glockenspiel, marimba, crotales

Publishing information: BOOSEY AND HAWKES. Pocket score for sale; full score (244 pp) and parts for hire.

Recording details:

First performance: February 26 1981

       at: Symphony Hall, Boston, Massachusetts

       by: Boston Symphony Orchestra, conducted by Seiji Ozawa

Notes: Commissioned by the Boston Symphony Orchestra to celebrate its centenary. A tape recording is available at the National Sound Archive for private study only.

FAREWELL TO STROMNESS
(arrangement)   **(1980)**

Catalogue no.:   J171

Descriptive title: FAREWELL   TO   STROMNESS.
                                  Arranged for guitar by Timothy Walker.

Musical format: Guitar solo

Location of manuscript: Timothy Walker

Analysis:

Performance length: 4 minutes

Composed: 1980   **Revised:**

Instruments: Guitar

Publishing information: BOOSEY AND HAWKES. Score (4 pp)
                                   for sale.

Recording details: HYPERION: Record, A 66027.
                                   Timothy Walker, guitar.

First performance: June 23 1980

           at: St. Magnus Festival, Kirkwall, Orkney

           by: Timothy Walker, guitar

Notes: Originally one of the piano interludes from *The Yellow
                      Cake Review*. See [J165] and [J166].

MEDIUM   (1981)

Catalogue no.:   J172

Descriptive title: THE MEDIUM.   Monodrama for
                                mezzo-soprano.

Musical format: Mezzo-soprano solo

Location of manuscript:

Analysis:

Performance length: 50 minutes

Composed: 1981   **Revised:**

Instruments: Mezzo-soprano

Publishing information: BOOSEY AND HAWKES.   Full score
                                (24 pp) for sale.

Recording details:

First performance: June 21 1981

    at: St. Magnus Festival, Kirkwall, Orkney

    by: Mary Thomas, mezzo-soprano.   Produced by David
                                 William.

Notes: Text by the composer.   A tape recording is available
                                 at the National Sound Archive for private study only.

PIANO SONATA   (1981)

Catalogue no.:   J173

Descriptive title:	PIANO SONATA
Musical format:	Piano solo
Location of manuscript:	Stephen Pruslin

Analysis: (i) *Sostenuto - allegro ma non troppo* (ii) *Scherzo - vivace* (iii) *Larghetto* (iv) *Cantabile con moto* (v) *Grave* (vi) *Scherzo - allegro molto* (vii) *Allegro preciso - adagio*

Performance length:	32 minutes

Composed: 1981   **Revised:**

Instruments: Piano

Publishing information:	CHESTER MUSIC. Score (41 pp) for sale.
Recording details:	AURACLE. Record, AUC 1005. Stephen Pruslin, piano. CD in preparation. Richard Holzman, piano.
First performance:	May 23 1981

      at: Bath Festival

      by: Stephen Pruslin, piano

Notes: This work has an admitted predecessor: Beethoven's Op. 110 in A flat, to which it sometimes refers.

RAINBOW   (1981)

Catalogue no.:   J174

Descriptive title: THE RAINBOW: Short music theatre work for young children to sing and play.

Musical format: Children's opera

Location of manuscript: Mrs Judy Arnold

Analysis: One act

Performance length: 25 minutes

Composed: 1981   **Revised:**

Instruments: Descant recorder, treble recorder, tenor recorder, solo violin, piano

Percussion (6 players): *I* - soprano glockenspiel

II - alto glockenspiel

III - chime bars, bicycle bell, klaxon

IV - wood block, tambourine, castanet

V - suspended cymbal, wood block, temple block

VI - bass drum, tam-tam (or gong)

Publishing information: BOOSEY AND HAWKES.   Teacher's score, choral score (76 pp) and set of instrumental parts for sale and hire. German translation available on request.

Recording details:

conitnued ...

First performance: June 20 1981

    at: St. Magnus Festival, Kirkwall, Orkney

    by: Pupils of Stromness Primary School, conducted by Janet Helsall. Produced by Jan MacLeod.

Notes: Text by the composer. The work is intended for children of ages 8 - 12. All singing parts are written in the treble clef, and are intended for unbroken boys' or girls' voices. The vocal line is always doubled by instruments. A tape recording is available at the National Sound Archive for private study only.

HILL RUNES   (1981)

Catalogue no.:   J175

Descriptive title: HILL RUNES for guitar

Musical format: Guitar solo

Location of manuscript: S.M.I.C. (MS)

Analysis: Five linked sections

Performance length: 9 minutes

Composed: 1981   **Revised:**

Instruments: Guitar

Publishing information: BOOSEY AND HAWKES. Score (7 pp) for sale.

Recording details: RCA RED SEAL: Record, RL 25419; Cassette, RK 25419. Julian Bream, guitar.

First performance: July 25th 1981

    at: Dartington Summer School

    by: Julian Bream, guitar

Notes:

BAIRNS OF BRUGH   (1981)

Catalogue no.:   J176

Descriptive title: THE BAIRNS OF BRUGH for ensemble

Musical format: Sextet

Location of manuscript: Eva Bergh, Bergen, Norway (widow
                                of Sverre Bergh)

Analysis: One continuous movement

Performance length: 6 minutes

Composed: 1981   **Revised:**

Instruments: Piccolo, bass clarinet, viola, cello, marimba, piano

Publishing information: BOOSEY AND HAWKES. Full score
                                (6 pp) for sale and hire; parts for hire.

Recording details: UNICORN-KANCHANA: CD, UK CD
                                2044; Cassette, DKP (C) 9033;
                                Record, DKP 9033.   The Fires of
                                London,   conducted   by   the
                                composer.

First performance: May 30 1981

    at: Bergen International Festival

    by: The Fires of London

Notes: For Sverre Bergh, in memoriam. The title refers to a
                    remote Orcadian archaeological site.

LITTLE QUARTET NO. 2   (1981)

Catalogue no.:   J177

Descriptive title: LITTLE QUARTET No. 2 for string quartet

Musical format: String quartet

Location of manuscript: Mrs Judy Arnold

Analysis: One continuous movement. *Adagio - allegro moderato, flessibile - adagio*

Performance length: 7 minutes

Composed: 1977   **Revised:**   1981

Instruments: String quartet

Publishing information: BOOSEY AND HAWKES. Score (20 pp in toto) and parts for sale (with *Little Quartet no. 1*) and hire.

Recording details:

First performance: November 12 1987

     at: St. Lawrence University, Canton, New York

     by: The Alexander Quartet

Notes: Commissioned by St. Lawrence University for the Alexander Quartet. The MS shows that the work was composed in 1977 but did not attain its present form until 1981. The revisions are extensive. See also *Little Quartet No. 1*, [J169]

SONATINA FOR TRUMPET   (1981)

Catalogue no.:   J178

Descriptive title: SONATINA FOR TRUMPET

Musical format: Trumpet

Location of manuscript: Boosey and Hawkes

Analysis: Three miniature movements, Fast - slow - fast

Performance length: $2\,^1/_2$ minutes

Composed: 1981   **Revised:**

Instruments: Trumpet

Publishing information: BOOSEY AND HAWKES. Score (2 pp) for sale in the volume *Contemporary Music for Trumpet* (12 pp in toto).

Recording details:

First performance:

    at:

    by:

Notes: Written as an instructive piece to prepare young trumpeters (Grade VIII) for what they might meet in the orchestral scores of Carter, Stockhausen or Maxwell Davies. A tape recording is available at the National Sound Archive for private study only.

LULLABYE FOR LUCY (1981)

Catalogue no.: J179

Descriptive title: LULLABYE FOR LUCY

Musical format: Unaccompanied chorus

Location of manuscript: S.M.I.C. (MS)

Analysis: *Adagio*

Performance length: 3 minutes

Composed: 1981 **Revised:**

Instruments: Soprano, Alto, Tenor and Bass chorus

Publishing information: BOOSEY AND HAWKES. Score (4 pp) for sale.

Recording details: UNICORN-KANCHANA: *A Celebration of Scotland* CD, DKP (CD) 9070; Cassette, DKP (C) 9070. St. Mary's School Choir, Edinburgh, conducted by the composer.

First performance: June 19 1981

at: St. Magnus Festival, Orkney

by: St. Magnus Singers, conducted by the composer

Notes: Text by George Mackay Brown. Written to celebrate the birth of a child in Rackwick on the island of Hoy. A tape recording is available at the National Sound Archive for private study only.

BRASS QUINTET   (1981)

Catalogue no.:   J180

Descriptive title: BRASS QUINTET

Musical format: Brass quintet

Location of manuscript: S.M.I.C. (MS)

Analysis: (i) *Adagio - allegro* (ii) *Adagio flessibile* (iii) *Allegro vivace*

Performance length: 25 minutes

Composed: 1981   **Revised:**

Instruments: Two trumpets, horn, trombone and tuba

Publishing information: Chester Music.   Study score (50 pp) and parts for sale separately.

Recording details:

First performance: March 19 1982

> **at:**   *Private*: Morse Auditorium, Boston
> *Public*: Town Hall, New York

> **by:**   Empire Brass Quintet

Notes: Commissioned by the Harvard Musical Association on behalf of the Empire Brass Quintet, recipients of the Association's 1980 Award. A tape recording is available at the National Sound Archive for private study only.

SEVEN SONGS HOME (1981)

Catalogue no.: J181

Descriptive title: SEVEN SONGS HOME for children's voices

Musical format: Unaccompanied children's chorus

Location of manuscript: S.M.I.C. (MS)

Analysis: (i) Home-time at last (ii) At the shore (iii) The heather track (iv) At the lochan (v) Old tractor (vi) Tractor ride (vii) Home

Performance length: 12 minutes

Composed: 1981 **Revised:**

Instruments: Children's voices, SAA

Publishing information: CHESTER MUSIC. Score (22 pp) for sale.

Recording details: UNICORN-KANCHANA: *A Celebration of Scotland* CD, DKP (CD) 9070; Cassette, DKP (C) 9070. St. Mary's School Choir, Edinburgh, conducted by the composer.

First performance: December 13 1982

at: Congress Hall, Academy of Sciences, Budapest

by: Children's Choir of Miskola Music Primary School Number 6, conducted by János Remenvi.

Notes: Commissioned by the International Kodály Society for the centenary of Zoltan Kodály's birth. Text by the composer. A tape recording is available at the National Sound Archive for private study only.

SONGS OF HOY   (1981)

Catalogue no.:   J182

Descriptive title: SONGS OF HOY for children to sing and play

Musical format: Children's opera

Location of manuscript: S.M.I.C. (MS)

Analysis: (i) Introduction (ii) Old Widow Grumble (action song) (iii) Islander's Home (iv) Our Family (action song) (v) Long Hope (instruments alone) (vi) Don't Look Now (action song) (vii) Rackwick Bay (viii) Home-time

Performance length: 25 minutes

Composed: 1981   **Revised:**

Instruments: Piano, descant recorders, guitar (optional)
Untuned percussion (4 players): side drum, bass drum, suspended cymbal, flexatone, tambourine, two wood blocks, maracas and castanets
Tuned percussion (optional): instruments such as glockenspiel, xylophone and chime bars may be used when available and where appropriate

Publishing information: CHESTER MUSIC. Teacher's score (35 pp), set of 10 voice parts and set of instrumental parts for sale.

Recording details:

First performance: June 21 1982

    at: St. Magnus Festival, Orkney

    by: Children of North Walls Primary School, conducted by Glenys Hughes

continued ...

Notes: Written for the children of Lyness School, Hoy, Orkney. Text by the composer. References to Hoy are incidental and may be adapted to suit the locality of any particular performance. Voices are in unison and always doubled. The intended age of performers is 8 to 12.

SEA EAGLE   (1982)

Catalogue no.:   J183

Descriptive title:	SEA EAGLE for horn
Musical format:	Horn solo
Location of manuscript:	S.M.I.C. (MS)

Analysis: (i) *Adagio* (ii) *Lento* (iii) *Presto molto*

Performance length:	9 minutes
Composed: 1982	**Revised:**
Instruments: Horn	
Publishing information:	CHESTER MUSIC. Score (4 pp) for sale.

Recording details:

First performance: August 16 1982

    at: Dartington Summer School

    by: Richard Watkins, horn

Notes: A tape recording is available at the National Sound Archive for private study only.

IMAGE, REFLECTION, SHADOW (1982)

Catalogue no.: J184

Descriptive title: IMAGE, REFLECTION, SHADOW for ensemble

Musical format: Sextet

Location of manuscript: S.M.I.C. (MS)

Analysis: (i) *Adagio* (ii) *Allegro* (iii) *Lento - allegro*

Performance length: 38 minutes

Composed: 1982 **Revised:**

Instruments: Flute (doubling piccolo and alto flute), clarinet in A (doubling bass clarinet), cimbalom, violin, cello, piano

Publishing information: CHESTER MUSIC. Miniature score (99 pp) for sale; full score and parts for hire.

Recording details: UNICORN-KANCHANA: CD, UK CD 2038; Cassette, DKP (C) 9033; Record, DKP 9033. The Fires of London, conducted by the composer.

First performance: August 22 1982

at: Municipal Theatre of Lucerne, Lucerne International Festival

by: Gregory Knowles (cimbalom) and the Fires of London

Notes: A companion piece to *Ave Maris Stella* [J131] with the marimba replaced by the cimbalom. The title does not refer to the three movements but to the play of mirror and copy, mainly in the writing for three duos of strings, percussion and woodwind.

SINFONIA CONCERTANTE   (1982)

Catalogue no.:   J185

Descriptive title: SINFONIA CONCERTANTE

Musical format: Chamber orchestra

Location of manuscript: S.M.I.C. (MS)

Analysis: (i) *Allegro molto* (ii) *Andante* (iii) *Flessibile*

Performance length: 30 minutes

Composed: 1982   **Revised:**

Instruments: Flute, oboe, clarinet, bassoon, horn, timpani, strings

Publishing information: CHESTER MUSIC.   Pocket score (76pp) for sale; full score and parts for sale.

Recording details: UNICORN-KANCHANA: CD, UK (CD) 2026; Cassette, DKP (C) 9058; Record, DKP 9058.   Scottish Chamber Orchestra, conducted by the composer.

First performance: August 12 1983

at: BBC Promenade Concert at the Royal Albert Hall, London

by: Academy of St. Martin-in-the-Fields, conducted by Sir Neville Marriner

Notes: Commissioned by the Academy of St. Martin-in-the-Fields.

ORGAN SONATA   (1982)

Catalogue no.:   J186

Descriptive title: ORGAN SONATA

Musical format: Organ solo

Location of manuscript: S.M.I.C. (MS); a pencil sketch is in the
                                  National Library of Scotland, Edinburgh

Analysis: Four movements

Performance length: 17 minutes

Composed: 1982   **Revised:**

Instruments: Organ

Publishing information: CHESTER MUSIC. Score (28 pp) for
                                  sale.

Recording details: MUSICA NOVA. CD in preparation.
                                  Gerald Willis, organ.

First performance: June 23 1982

           at: St. Magnus Festival, Orkney

           by: Richard Hughes, organ

Notes: Written for Richard Hughes. Each movement is
                  developed from a fragment of plainsong from the
                  Maundy Thursday office. A tape recording is available
                  at the National Sound Archive for private study only.

TALLIS: FOUR VOLUNTARIES   (1982)

Catalogue no.:   J187

Descriptive title: TALLIS: FOUR VOLUNTARIES
arranged for brass quintet

Musical format: Brass quintet

Location of manuscript: S.M.I.C. (MS and sketch)

Analysis: (i) *Veni redemptor gentium I* (ii) *Ex more docti mistico* (iii) *Ecce tempus idoneum* (iv) *Veni redemptor gentium II*

Performance length: 5 minutes

Composed: 1982   **Revised:**

Instruments: Two trumpets, horn, trombone, tuba

Publishing information: CHESTER MUSIC. Full score (4 pp) for sale; parts for sale and hire.

Recording details:

First performance: December 9 1983

    at: The Cloisters, New York

    by: The Empire Brass Quintet

Notes: A straight arrangement of organ pieces. An arrangement for brass band has also been made (see following entry, [J188]).

TALLIS: FOUR VOLUNTARIES　　(1982)

Catalogue no.:　J188

Descriptive title:　　　TALLIS: FOUR VOLUNTARIES arranged for brass band

Musical format:　　　Brass band

Location of manuscript:

Analysis:　　　(i) *Veni redemptor gentium I* (ii) *Ex more docti mistico* (iii) *Ecce tempus idoneum* (iv) *Veni redemptor gentium II*

Performance length:　　　5 minutes

Composed:　1982　　　**Revised:**　1983

Instruments:　Soprano cornet, solo cornet, three cornets, French horn, three tenor horns, two baritones, two euphoniums, two trombones, bass trombone, two E flat basses, two B B flat basses

Publishing information:　　　CHESTER MUSIC. Full score and parts for hire.

Recording details:

First performance:　　　June 17 1983

　　at:　Papdale Infants School, Kirkwall, Orkney at the St. Magnus Festival

　　by:　Orkney Youth Brass Band, conducted by John V. Jones

Notes:　This is a brass band arrangement of the previous entry, [J187].

GESUALDO: TWO MOTETS   (1982)

Catalogue no.:   J189

Descriptive title: GESUALDO: TWO MOTETS arranged for brass quintet

Musical format: Brass quintet

Location of manuscript: S.M.I.C. (MS and sketch)

Analysis: (i) *Peccantem me quotidie* (ii) *O vos omnes*

Performance length: 5 minutes

Composed: 1982   **Revised:**

Instruments: Two trumpets, horn, trombone, tuba

Publishing information: CHESTER MUSIC. Full score (5 pp) and parts separately available for sale and hire.

Recording details:

First performance: August 18 1983

    at: Dartington Summer School

    by: Albany Brass Ensemble

Notes: A transcription of music from the volume of motets in 5 voices which Gesualdo published in 1603. Davies' transcriptions are straight except for the addition of dynamic markings. There is also a brass band arrangement; see next entry, [J190].

GESUALDO: TWO MOTETS   (1982)

Catalogue no.:   J190

Descriptive title: GESUALDO: TWO MOTETS arranged for brass band

Musical format: Brass band

Location of manuscript:

Analysis: (i) *Peccantem me quotidie* (ii) *O vos omnes*

Performance length: 5 minutes

Composed: 1982   **Revised:**

Instruments: Soprano cornet, solo cornet, three cornets, flugel horn, three tenor horns, two baritones, two euphoniums, two tenor trombones, bass trombone, two E flat basses, 2 BB flat basses

Publishing information: CHESTER MUSIC. Full score and parts separately available for sale.

Recording details:

First performance:

     at:

     by:

Notes: This is a brass band arrangement of the previous entry, [J189].

MARCH: THE POLE STAR (1982)

Catalogue no.:   J191

Descriptive title: MARCH: THE POLE STAR for brass quintet

Musical format: Brass quintet

Location of manuscript: S.M.I.C. (MS and sketch)

Analysis:

Performance length: 4 minutes

Composed: 1982   **Revised:**

Instruments: Two trumpets, horn, trombone, tuba

Publishing information: CHESTER MUSIC. Full score (6 pp) and parts separately for sale.

Recording details: MERLIN: Record, MRF 86041. Fine Arts Brass Ensemble.

First performance: August 18 1983

      at: Dartington Summer School

      by: The Albany Brass Ensemble

Notes: An arrangement for brass band has also been made; see next entry, [J192].

MARCH: THE POLE STAR   (1982)

Catalogue no.:   J192

Descriptive title: MARCH: THE POLE STAR for brass
                                  band

Musical format: Brass band

Location of manuscript:

Analysis:

Performance length: 4 minutes

Composed: 1982   **Revised:**

Instruments: Soprano cornet, solo cornet, two cornets, French horn,
                    three tenor horns, two baritones, two euphoniums, two
                    tenor trombones, bass trombone, two E flat basses, two
                    B B flat basses

Publishing information: CHESTER MUSIC. Full score and parts
                                   separately for sale and hire.

Recording details:

First performance: June 20 1983

    at: St. Magnus' Cathedral, Orkney, at the St. Magnus Festival

    by: Stromness Academy Brass, conducted by John V. Jones

Notes: An arrangement of the brass quintet piece; see previous
              entry, [J191].

BIRTHDAY MUSIC FOR JOHN   (1983)

Catalogue no.:   J193

Descriptive title: BIRTHDAY MUSIC FOR JOHN for flute, viola and cello

Musical format: Flute, viola and cello

Location of manuscript: John Carewe

Analysis: (i) *Allegro* (ii) *Adagio* (iii) *Allegro*

Performance length: 9 minutes

Composed: 1983   **Revised:**

Instruments: Flute, viola, cello

Publishing information: CHESTER MUSIC. Miniature score (9 pp) and parts available separately for sale.

Recording details:

First performance: October 13 1983

      at: Swansea Festival

      by: Members of the Fires of London

Notes: 'John' is John Carewe, a conductor associated with the composer's music since the 1950s; the piece was a 50th birthday present. This piece was originally written in two movements, but a third was added later. The first complete performance is given above, but a private performance of the first two movements was given on January 25 1983.

INTO THE LABYRINTH   (1983)

Catalogue no.:   J194

Descriptive title: INTO THE LABYRINTH. Cantata for tenor and chamber orchestra

Musical format: Voice(s) and orchestra

Location of manuscript: S.M.I.C. (MS)

Analysis: (i) *Lento* (ii) *Allegro* (iii) *Lento* (iv) *Adagio* (v) *Andante* (played without a break)

Performance length: 30 minutes

Composed: 1983   **Revised:**

Instruments: Tenor, two flutes, two oboes, two clarinets, two bassoons, two horns, two trumpets, strings

Publishing information: CHESTER MUSIC. Pocket score (74pp) for sale; full score and parts for sale.

Recording details: UNICORN-KANCHANA: CD, UK (CD) 2022; Cassette, DKP (C) 9038; Record, DKP 9038. Neil Mackie, tenor and the Scottish Chamber Orchestra, conducted by the composer.

First performance: June 22 1983

    at: St. Magnus Festival in St. Magnus' Cathedral, Kirkwall, Orkney

    by: Neil Mackie, tenor and the Scottish Chamber Orchestra, conducted by James Conlon

Notes: Commissioned by the Scottish Chamber Orchestra. The text is taken from the play *The Well* by George Mackay Brown.

SINFONIETTA ACCADEMICA   (1983)

Catalogue no.:   J195

Descriptive title: SINFONIETTA ACCADEMICA

Musical format: Full orchestra

Location of manuscript: S.M.I.C. (MS)

Analysis: (i) *Allegro moderato* (ii) *Largo* (iii) *Andante*

Performance length: 32 minutes

Composed: 1983   **Revised:**

Instruments: Two flutes, two oboes, two clarinets, two bassoons, two horns, two trumpets, strings

Publishing information: CHESTER MUSIC.   Pocket score (106 pp) for sale; full score and parts for hire.

Recording details: UNICORN-KANCHANA: CD, UK (CD) 2022; Cassette, DKP (C) 9038; Record, DKP 9038.   The Scottish Chamber Orchestra, conducted by the composer.

First performance: October 6 1983

    at: Reid Hall, Edinburgh University

    by: The Scottish Chamber Orchestra, conducted by Edward Harper

Notes: Commissioned by Edinburgh University to celebrate its 400th anniversary.

WE MET IN ST. LOUIS (1983)

Catalogue no.:   J196

Descriptive title: WE MET IN ST. LOUIS - A BIRTHDAY
                               CARD

Musical format: Solo cello (not indicated)

Location of manuscript: Mrs Judy Arnold (MS)

Analysis: *Adagio*

Performance length:

Composed: 1983   **Revised:**

Instruments: Cello

Publishing information: MS

Recording details:

First performance:

       at:

       by:

Notes: Marked "Greetings to Jonathan [Williams] from Max,
                 St. Louis, November 19 1983".

AGNUS DEI   (1984)

Catalogue no.:   J197

Descriptive title: AGNUS DEI.   Motet for two solo
                                sopranos, viola and cello (see Notes)

Musical format: Voice(s) and instruments

Location of manuscript: S.M.I.C. (MS)

Analysis:

Performance length: 5 minutes

Composed: 1984   **Revised:**

Instruments: Two solo sopranos, viola and cello

Publishing information: CHESTER MUSIC. Full score and parts
                                for sale separately.

Recording details:

First performance: June 23 1986

    at: Almeida Festival, London

    by: Members of the Almeida Festival Players, conducted
                                by Oliver Knussen

Notes: Motet for two sopranos or two trebles or soprano or
                                treble choir divided into two plus viola and cello.

SONATINE   (1984)

Catalogue no.:   J198

Descriptive title: SONATINE for violin and cimbalom
Musical format: Violin and cimbalom
Location of manuscript: Mrs Judy Arnold
Analysis: (i) *Lento - allegro* (ii) *Presto* (iii) Lullaby - *adagio*
Performance length: 12 minutes
Composed: 1984   **Revised:**
Instruments: Violin, cimbalom
Publishing information: CHESTER MUSIC.   Miniature score (14 pp) and parts for sale.

Recording details:

First performance: June 8 1984

at: Wigmore Hall, London

by: Rosemary Furniss, violin and Gregory Knowles, cimbalom

Notes: Written as a wedding present for Rosemary Furniss and Gregory Knowles of the Fires of London.

page 231

UNBROKEN CIRCLE   (1984)

Catalogue no.:   J199

Descriptive title:	UNBROKEN CIRCLE for ensemble
Musical format:	Quintet
Location of manuscript:	Sir William Glock

Analysis: One continuous movement

Performance length: 5 minutes

Composed: 1984   **Revised:**

Instruments: Alto flute, bass clarinet, viola, cello, piano

Publishing information: CHESTER MUSIC.   Miniature score (9 pp) and parts on sale separately.

Recording details:

First performance: November 30 1984

    at: The Cultural Centre, Rennes

    by: The Fires of London, conducted by the composer

Notes: Composed in homage to Sir William Glock. A private performance took place on June 3 1984 in the Bath Assembly Rooms; the piece was played by the London Sinfonietta, conducted by Diego Masson.

No. 11 BUS   (1984)

Catalogue no.:   J200

Descriptive title: THE No. 11 BUS. Music theatre work
                                for tenor, mezzo-soprano, baritone, two
                                dancers, mime and ensemble

Musical format: Voice(s) and instruments

Location of manuscript: S.M.I.C. (MS)

Analysis: One continuous movement

Performance length: 50 minutes

Composed: 1984   **Revised:**

Instruments: Mime, two dancers, Mezzo-soprano, Tenor, Baritone,
                  flute (doubling piccolo), clarinet in A (doubling
                  clarinet in B flat and bass clarinet), violin, cello, piano
                  (doubling celesta)
                  Percussion (1 player): marimba, crotales, snare drum,
                  bass drum (with foot pedal), five bongos, two
                  tom-toms, small and large suspended cymbals, small
                  Chinese suspended cymbal, choke cymbal, tam-tam,
                  tambourine, small tambourine, sleighbells, saucepan,
                  wood block, lion's roar, police whistle, rubber plunger
                  and plastic bucket, rock band kit, clarioline

Publishing information: CHESTER MUSIC. Miniature score and
                                libretto with German translation (104 pp)
                                for sale; full score, vocal score and parts
                                for hire.

Recording details:

First performance: March 20 1984

> **at:** Queen Elizabeth Hall, London

> **by:** Simon McBurney, mime, Anne Dickie and Tom Yang, dancers, Mary Thomas, mezzo-soprano, Donald Stephenson, tenor, Brian Rayner Cook, baritone and the Fires of London, conducted by Günther Bauer-Schenk. Directed by Brenda McLean.

Notes: Dedicated to Michael and Judy Arnold. Libretto by the composer. The conductor and six instrumentalists are all involved in the stage action and are therefore in costume.

GUITAR SONATA   (1984)

Catalogue no.:   J201

Descriptive title: GUITAR SONATA

Musical format: Guitar solo

Location of manuscript: S.M.I.C. (MS)

Analysis: (i) *Andante, recitando* (ii) *Lento* (iii) *Allegro*

Performance length: 10 minutes

Composed: 1984   **Revised:**

Instruments: Guitar

Publishing information: CHESTER MUSIC. Score for sale and hire.

Recording details: NEW ALBION RECORDS: CD in preparation. David Tannenbaum, guitar.

First performance: June 20 1987

    at: St. Magnus Festival, Orkney

    by: Timothy Walker, guitar

Notes:

ONE STAR AT LAST   (1984)

Catalogue no.:   J202

Descriptive title: ONE STAR AT LAST. Carol for SATB
                                chorus.

Musical format: Unaccompanied chorus

Location of manuscript: S.M.I.C. (MS)

Analysis:

Performance length: 4 minutes

Composed: 1984   **Revised:**

Instruments: Soprano, Alto, Tenor and Bass chorus

Publishing information: CHESTER MUSIC.   Score (7 pp) for
                                     sale in *The Chester Book of Christmas
                                     Carols* (102 pp in toto).

Recording details:

First performance: December 24 1984

      at: King's College, Cambridge, in the service of nine lessons
                                and carols

      by: King's College Choir, conducted by Stephen Cleobury

Notes: The text is from a poem by George Mackay Brown. A
                    tape recording is available at the National Sound
                    Archive for private study only.

SYMPHONY NO. 3 (1984)

Catalogue no.: J203

Descriptive title: SYMPHONY NO. 3

Musical format: Full orchestra

Location of manuscript: Mrs Judy Arnold

Analysis: (i) *Lento - allegro al breve* (ii) *Scherzo I - allegro* (iii) *Scherzo II - allegro vivace* (iv) *Lento*

Performance length: 50 minutes

Composed: 1984 **Revised:**

Instruments: Three flutes (with piccolo and alto doublings), two oboes, cor anglais, two clarinets, bass clarinet, two bassoons, contrabassoon, four horns, three trumpets, two trombones, bass trombone, tuba, timpani and strings

Publishing information: BOOSEY AND HAWKES. Pocket score (266 pp) for sale; full score and parts for hire.

Recording details: BBC RECORDS: CD, BBC CD 560 X; Record, REGL 560. BBC Philharmonic Orchestra, conducted by Edward Downes.

First performance: February 19 1985

at: Free Trade Hall, Manchester

by: BBC Philharmonic Orchestra, conducted by Edward Downes

Notes: Commissioned by the BBC Philharmonic Orchestra to celebrate its 50th anniversary.

MUSIC IN OUR TIME   (?1985)

Catalogue no.:   J204

Descriptive title: MUSIC IN OUR TIME: OPENING
                                SEQUENCE

Musical format:

Location of manuscript:

Analysis:

Performance length:

Composed: ?1985   **Revised:**

Instruments:

Publishing information: MS

Recording details:

First performance:

      at:

      by:

Notes: Written for the BBC2 series.

ORKNEY WEDDING, WITH SUNRISE (1985)

Catalogue no.: J205

Descriptive title: AN ORKNEY WEDDING, WITH SUNRISE

Musical format: Full orchestra

Location of manuscript: S.M.I.C. (MS)

Analysis: One continuous movement

Performance length: 12 minutes

Composed: 1985 **Revised:**

Instruments: Two flutes, two oboes, two clarinets (second doubling bass clarinet), two bassoons, four horns, two trumpets, two trombones, tuba, timpani, highland bagpipes, strings
Percussion (4 players): *I* - cymbals, tambourine
II - swannee whistle, wood block, glockenspiel
III - slapstick, side drum, marimba, crotales
IV - bass drum

Publishing information: BOOSEY AND HAWKES. Pocket score (65 pp) for sale; full score and parts for hire.

Recording details: UNICORN-KANCHANA: *A Celebration of Scotland* CD, DKP (CD) 9070; Cassette, DKP (C) 9070. George Macllwham, highland bagpipes and the Scottish Chamber Orchestra, conducted by the composer.
PHILIPS: CD, *Pops Britannia* 420946-2. Nancy Tunnicliffe and the Boston Pops Orchestra, conducted by John Williams.

continued ...

First performance: May 10 1985

    at: Symphony Hall, Boston, Massachusetts

    by: Boston Pops Orchestra, conducted by John Williams

Notes: Commissioned by the Boston Pops Orchestra to celebrate its centenary. A tape recording is available at the National Sound Archive for private study only.

FIRST FERRY TO HOY　　　　　(1985)

Catalogue no.:　　J206

Descriptive title:　　FIRST FERRY TO HOY for junior SATB chorus, junior percussion and recorder band and ensemble

Musical format:　　Voice(s) and instruments

Location of manuscript:　　S.M.I.C. (MS)

Analysis:　　(i) Introduction (ii) The town wakes up (iii) Early morning townscape (iv) At the pier (v) The boat ride, close in shore (vi) Out at sea (vii) The sea with whales (viii) Loss (ix) Epilogue

Performance length:　　16 minutes

Composed:　　1985　　　**Revised:**

Instruments:　　Flute (doubling alto flute), oboe, clarinet, bassoon, horn, trumpet, trombone, celesta, violin I, violin II, viola, cello, double bass

Percussion (1 player): glockenspiel, crotales, bell-tree, bass drum

Children's recorder band: descant I, descant II, treble, tenor

Children's percussion band (20 players): two glockenspiels, two chime bars, four xylophones, four metallophones, castanets, maracas, tambourine, side drum, bass drum, suspended cymbal, clashed cymbals, tam-tam

Publishing information:　　BOOSEY AND HAWKES. Full score (76 pp) and children's band parts for sale and hire; choral score for sale; parts and professional instrumental parts for hire.

Recording details:

continued ...

First performance:　　　　November 12 1985

    at: Queen Elizabeth Hall, London

    by: The London Sinfonietta, ILEA Youth Choir and ILEA Children's Band, conducted by Elgar Howarth

Notes: Commissioned by the London Sinfonietta. The text is by the composer.

PEAT CUTTERS   (1985)

Catalogue no.:   J207

Descriptive title: THE PEAT CUTTERS for brass band, SATB youth chorus and children's chorus

Musical format: Voice(s) and instruments

Location of manuscript: S.M.I.C. (MS)

Analysis: (i) The eagle (ii) The fire (iii) St. Francis (iv) Poor philosophy (v) A black resurrection

Performance length: 25 minutes

Composed: 1985   **Revised:**

Instruments: Soprano, Alto, Tenor and Bass youth chorus, children's chorus, soprano cornet, solo cornet, two cornets, flugelhorn, three tenor horns, two baritones, two euphoniums, two trombones, bass trombone, two E flat basses, two B B flat basses

Publishing information: BOOSEY AND HAWKES. Full score and choral score for sale and hire; brass band parts for hire. Vocal score (36 pp) for sale.

Recording details:

First performance: August 18 1985

at: Usher Hall, Edinburgh, at the Edinburgh International Festival

by: Scottish Youth Brass Band, and the Junior Choir of the Scottish National Orchestra, conducted by Geoffrey Brand

Notes: Commissioned by the Carnegie Trust (UK) Ltd. The text is by the composer; it is on the renewal of nature and the need to take care of the earth. The vocal line is doubled by instruments.

VIOLIN CONCERTO (1985)

Catalogue no.:   J208

Descriptive title:	CONCERTO FOR VIOLIN AND ORCHESTRA
Musical format:	Violin and orchestra
Location of manuscript:	S.M.I.C. (MS)

Analysis: (i) *Allegro moderato* (ii) *Adagio* (iii) *Allegro non troppo*

Performance length: 30 minutes

Composed: 1985   **Revised:**

Instruments: Violin solo, two flutes, two oboes, two clarinets in A, two bassoons, two horns, two trumpets in C, timpani and strings

Publishing information: CHESTER MUSIC. Pocket score for sale; full score (112 pp), parts and a piano reduction with violin for hire.

Recording details: CBS: CD, MK 42449; Cassette, MT 42449; Record, M 42449. Isaac Stern, violin and the Royal Philharmonia Orchestra, conducted by Andre Previn.

First performance: June 21 1986

at: St. Magnus' Cathedral, Kirkwall, Orkney, for the 10th St. Magnus Festival

by: Isaac Stern, violin and the Royal Philharmonic Orchestra, conducted by Andre Previn

Notes: Commissioned by the Royal Philharmonic Orchestra to celebrate their 40th anniversary. A tape recording is available at the National Sound Archive for private study only.

JIMMACK THE POSTIE (1986)

Catalogue no.: J209

Descriptive title: JIMMACK THE POSTIE: Overture for orchestra

Musical format: Full orchestra

Location of manuscript: Ian Barr

Analysis: One continuous movement

Performance length: 9 minutes

Composed: 1986 **Revised:**

Instruments: Two flutes (first doubling piccolo, second doubling alto flute), two oboes, two bassoons, two horns, two trumpets in C, two trombones, timpani and strings

Publishing information: CHESTER MUSIC. Pocket score for sale; full score (45 pp) and parts for hire.

Recording details: UNICORN-KANCHANA: *A Celebration of Scotland* CD, DKP (CD) 9070; Cassette, DKP (C) 9070. The Scottish Chamber Orchestra, conducted by the composer.

First performance: June 22 1986

at: Phoenix Cinema, Kirkwall, Orkney for the 10th St. Magnus Festival

by: The Royal Philharmonic Orchestra, conducted by the composer

Notes: Commissioned by Ian Barr for the Scottish Post Office. Ian Barr was Chairman of the Scottish Post Office at the time the pice was written.

HOUSE OF WINTER   (1986)

Catalogue no.:   J210

Descriptive title: HOUSE OF WINTER. Song cycle for vocal sextet or AATBBB chorus

Musical format: Unaccompanied chorus

Location of manuscript: S.M.I.C. (MS)

Analysis:

Performance length: 12 minutes

Composed: 1986   **Revised:**

Instruments: Alto I, Alto II, Tenor, Bass I, Bass II and Bass III *or* Soprano, Alto, Tenor, Bass I, Bass II and Bass III soloists *or* chorus

Publishing information: CHESTER MUSIC. Score (20 pp) for sale.

Recording details:

First performance: June 23 1986

      at: East Kirk, Kirkwall, Orkney, at the St. Magnus Festival

      by: The King's Singers

Notes: Commissioned by the King's Singers. The text is from English poems by George Mackay Brown. A tape recording is available at the National Sound Archive for private study only.

SEA RUNES

(1986)

Catalogue no.:   J211

Descriptive title: SEA RUNES for vocal sextet or AATBBB chorus

Musical format: Unaccompanied chorus

Location of manuscript: S.M.I.C. (MS)

Analysis: (i) Five crags (ii) Elder (iii) Croft-fisherman (iv) Shopkeeper (v) New boat (vi) Fishmonger

Performance length: 3 minutes

Composed: 1986   **Revised:**

Instruments: Alto I, Alto II, Tenor, Bass I, Bass II and Bass III *or* Soprano, Alto, Tenor, Bass I, Bass II and Bass III soloists *or* chorus

Publishing information: CHESTER MUSIC. Score (12 pp) for sale.

Recording details:

First performance: November 16 1986

at: Alice Tully Hall, Lincoln Center, New York

by: The King's Singers

Notes: Commissioned by the King's Singers. The text is from an English poem by George Mackay Brown.

EXCUSE ME   (1986)

Catalogue no.:   J212

Descriptive title: EXCUSE ME for voice and ensemble

Musical format: Voice(s) and instruments

Location of manuscript: S.M.I.C. (MS)

Analysis: (i) John and Jean (ii) Reason in Madness (iii) Excuse
me (iv) Grog

Performance length: 20 minutes

Composed: 1986   **Revised:**

Instruments: Mezzo-soprano, flute, clarinet in B flat, clarinet in A,
violin, cello, piano
Percussion (1 player): glockenspiel, marimba, bass
drum, suspended cymbal, two wood blocks, two
temple blocks

Publishing information: CHESTER MUSIC. Full score (43 pp)
and parts for hire.

Recording details:

First performance: February 26 1986

    at: Queen Elizabeth Hall, London

    by: Mary Thomas, mezzo-soprano and the Fires of London,
conducted by Nicholas Cleobury

Notes: An arrangement of four parlour songs by Charles Dibdin
(1740 - 1814).

DOWLAND: FAREWELL - A FANCYE

(1986)

Catalogue no.: J213

Descriptive title: DOWLAND: FAREWELL - A FANCYE. Realisation for ensemble

Musical format: Sextet

Location of manuscript: Mrs Judy Arnold

Analysis: One continuous movement

Performance length: 5 minutes

Composed: 1986 **Revised:**

Instruments: Alto flute, bass clarinet, viola, cello, marimba, piano

Publishing information: BOOSEY AND HAWKES. Full score (8 pp) and parts for hire.

Recording details:

First performance: January 20 1987

at: Queen Elizabeth Hall, London

by: The Fires of London, conducted by the composer

Notes: Written for the farewell concert of the Fires of London. Adapted from a lute fantasy by John Dowland.

WINTERFOLD   **(1986)**

Catalogue no.:   J214

Descriptive title: WINTERFOLD. Song cycle for mezzo-soprano and ensemble

Musical format: Voice(s) and instruments

Location of manuscript: North-Western University, Evanston, Illinois, USA

Analysis: One continuous movement

Performance length: 11 minutes

Composed: 1986   **Revised:**

Instruments: Mezzo-soprano, alto flute, bass clarinet, guitar, piano, viola, cello

Percussion (1 player): deep nipple gong, tam-tam, very small high claves, very large bass drum, tenor drum, marimba, crotales (two octaves, chromatic), glockenspiel, small suspended cymbal, bell tree, small high wood block

Publishing information: CHESTER MUSIC. Full score and parts for hire.

Recording details:

First performance: January 20 1987

    at: Queen Elizabeth Hall, London

    by: Mary Thomas, mezzo-soprano and the Fires of London, conducted by the composer

Notes: Text by George Mackay Brown.

STRATHCLYDE CONCERTO NO. 1 (1987)

Catalogue no.:   J215

Descriptive title: STRATHCLYDE CONCERTO NO. 1 for oboe and orchestra

Musical format: Oboe and orchestra

Location of manuscript: Mrs Judy Arnold

Analysis: (i) *Adagio molto - allegro moderato* (ii) *Adagio* (iii) *Allegro*

Performance length: 27 minutes

Composed: 1987   Revised:

Instruments: Oboe solo, two flutes, two clarinets in A, two horns, timpani, strings

Publishing information: BOOSEY AND HAWKES. Pocket score (60 pp) and a piano reduction with oboe part for sale; full score and parts for sale.

Recording details: UNICORN-KANCHANA: CD, DKP (CD) 9085; Cassette, DKP (C) 9085. Robin Miller, oboe and the Scottish Chamber Orchestra, conducted by the composer.

First performance: April 29 1988

at: City Hall, Glasgow

by: Robin Miller, oboe and the Scottish Chamber Orchestra, conducted by the composer

Notes: Commissioned jointly by Strathclyde Regional Council and the Scottish Chamber Orchestra with funds provided by the Scottish Arts Council and Strathclyde Regional Council. A tape recording is available at the National Sound Archive for private study only.

RESURRECTION (1987)

Catalogue no.: J216

Descriptive title: RESURRECTION, opera in one act with prologue

Musical format: Opera

Location of manuscript: Mrs Judy Arnold

Analysis: One act

Performance length: 70 minutes

Composed: 1987 **Revised:**

Instruments: Mezzo-soprano, Counter-tenor, two Tenors, two Baritones, Bass, minimum of five dancers, electronic vocal quartet (Soprano, Alto, Tenor, Bass, sound mixer)
Rock group: vocalist (male or female), melody instrument, two electronic keyboards, mallets, drums, electric bass guitar
Salvation Army band: two cornets, two trombones, tuba, bombardon, tambourine, cymbal (doubling bass drum)
Pit orchestra: flute (doubling piccolo and alto flute), oboe, clarinet in A (doubling clarinet in B flat and bass clarinet), alto saxophone, bassoon (doubling contrabassoon), horn, trumpet, trombone, guitar (doubling banjo and electric bass guitar), piano (doubling out-of-tune upright piano, celesta, Hammond organ), strings

continued ...

Percussion (2 players): *I* - small, medium and large suspended cymbals, small choke cymbal, hi-hat cymbal, high-domed Chinese cymbal, clashed cymbals, regular and small side drums, tenor drum, bass drum, tam-tam and plastic soap dish, bell tree, referee's whistle, tambourine, small altar bell, small wood block, two very small wood blocks, three very high wood blocks, four temple blocks, very small, high temple block, two pieces of wood covered with sandpaper, thunder sheet, slapstick, timpani, swannee whistle, heavy chains, cat-o'-nine-tails, jazz kit, balloon, bones

II - crotales, vibraphone, glockenspiel, marimba, timpani, tubular bells

Publishing information: CHESTER MUSIC. Full score (in English and German) (564 pp) and libretto for sale and hire; vocal score and parts for hire.

Recording details:

First performance: September 18 1987

   at: Stadtstheater, Darmstadt

   by: Stadtstheater, Darmstadt, conducted by Hans Drewanz, produced by Peter Brenner and designed by Waltraud Engelbert

Notes: Commissioned by the City of Darmstadt. Libretto by the composer.

MISHKENOT (1988)

Catalogue no.:   J217

Descriptive title: MISHKENOT for ensemble

Musical format: Nine instrumentalists

Location of manuscript: Mrs Judy Arnold

Analysis:

Performance length: 7 minutes

Composed: 1988   **Revised:**

Instruments: Flute (doubling piccolo), clarinet in A, horn, trumpet in C, violin, viola, cello
Percussion (1 player): glockenspiel, marimba, crotales (chromatic), very large bass drum

Publishing information: BOOSEY AND HAWKES. Full score for sale; parts for hire.

Recording details:

First performance: *Broadcast*: May 3 1988

    at: BBC Radio 3, as part of Sir William Glock's 80th birthday celebrations

    by: The London Sinfonietta, conducted by Elgar Howarth

Notes: Commissioned by the BBC for Sir William Glock's 80th birthday. Mishkenot is the name of the institute in Jerusalem where the piece was written.

STRATHCLYDE CONCERTO NO. 2   (1988)

Catalogue no.:   J218

Descriptive title: STRATHCLYDE CONCERTO NO. 2 for cello and orchestra

Musical format: Cello and orchestra

Location of manuscript: Mrs Judy Arnold

Analysis: (i) *Moderato* (ii) *Lento* (iii) *Allegro moderato*

Performance length: 37 minutes

Composed: 1988   **Revised:**

Instruments: Cello solo, two flutes (second doubling piccolo), two oboes, clarinet in A, bass clarinet, two bassoons, two horns, two trumpets in C, timpani, strings

Publishing information: CHESTER MUSIC.   Pocket score and piano reduction with cello part for sale; full score and parts for hire.

Recording details: UNICORN-KANCHANA: CD, DKP (CD) 9085; Cassette, DKP (C) 9085. William Conway, cello and the Scottish Chamber Orchestra, conducted by the composer.

First performance: February 1 1989

at: City Hall, Glasgow

by: William Conway, cello and the Scottish Chamber Ensemble, conducted by the composer

Notes: Commissioned jointly by Strathclyde Regional Council and the Scottish Chamber Orchestra with funds provided by the Scottish Arts Council and Strathclyde Regional Council, and dedicated to William Conway and the Scottish Chamber Orchestra. A tape recording is available at the National Sound Archive for private study only.

TRUMPET CONCERTO (1988)

Catalogue no.: J219

Descriptive title: CONCERTO FOR TRUMPET AND ORCHESTRA

Musical format: Trumpet and orchestra

Location of manuscript: Mrs Judy Arnold

Analysis: One continuous movement: *Adagio - allegro - adagio molto - presto - cadenza - lento*

Performance length: 28 minutes

Composed: 1988   **Revised:**

Instruments: Trumpet solo, two flutes, alto flute, cor anglais, two clarinets in A, bass clarinet in B flat, two bassoons, contrabassoon, four horns in F, three trumpets in C, three trombones, tuba, timpani, strings
Percussion (4 players): glockenspiel, marimba, crotales (two chromatic octaves), tambourine, bell tree, very large bass drum, Japanese temple gong

Publishing information: BOOSEY AND HAWKES. Pocket score (96 pp) and piano reduction with cello part for sale; full score and parts for hire.

Recording details: PHILIPS: CD (in preparation). Håkon Hardenberger, trumpet and the BBC Philharmonic Orchestra, conducted by Elgar Howarth.
COLLINS CLASSICS: CD and Cassette in preparation. John Wallace, trumpet and the Scottish Chamber Orchestra, conducted by the composer.

continued ...

First performance: September 21 1988

       at: The Yubin-Chokin Kaikan Hall, Hiroshima, Japan

       by: John Wallace, trumpet and the Philharmonia Orchestra, conducted by Giuseppe Sinopoli

Notes: Commissioned by the Philharmonia Orchestra with funds provided by the Arts Council. A tape recording is available at the National Sound Archive for private study only.

DANCES FROM
'THE TWO FIDDLERS' (1988)

Catalogue no.:   J220

Descriptive title:	DANCES FROM 'THE TWO FIDDLERS' arranged for violin and piano
Musical format:	Violin and piano
Location of manuscript:	Mrs Judy Arnold

Analysis:

Performance length: 6 $^1/_2$ minutes

Composed: 1978   **Revised:**   1988

Instruments: Violin, piano

Publishing information: BOOSEY AND HAWKES. Performing score (9 pp) with violin part (4 pp) for sale.

Recording details:

First performance: June 19 1988

      at: Stromness Academy, Orkney, for the St. Magnus Festival

      by: György Pauk, violin and Peter Frankl, piano

Notes: The music derives from Orkney fiddle tunes and was originally composed for the school opera *The Two Fiddlers*. See [J153] and [J154].

SIX SONGS FOR ST. ANDREW'S   (1988)

Catalogue no.:   **J221**

Descriptive title: SIX SONGS FOR ST. ANDREW'S. Song cycle for very young children to play and sing.

Musical format: Children's voice(s) and instruments

Location of manuscript: Mrs Judy Arnold

Analysis: (i) A Welcome Song (ii) Traffic Song (iii) A Song for Dinner-Time (a Round) (iv) Night (an IMAGINATION Song) (v) Circus Song (vi) Home-Time Song

Performance length: 15 minutes

Composed: 1988   **Revised:**

Instruments: Children's voices, recorders, tuned percussion
Unpitched percussion: tambourine, cymbals, bass drum, side drum, wood block I, wood block II

Publishing information: LONGMAN. Score for sale (Spring 1991).

Recording details:

First performance: June 18 1988

    at: Papdale Primary School, Kirkwall, Orkney, for the St. Magnus Festival

    by: Pupils of St. Andrew's School, conducted by Glenys Hughes

Notes: Text by the composer.

GREAT BANK ROBBERY (1989)

Catalogue no.: J222

Descriptive title: THE GREAT BANK ROBBERY. Music theatre work for children to play and sing.

Musical format: Children's opera

Location of manuscript: Mrs Judy Arnold

Analysis: Three scenes linked by instrumental sections: (i) The Bank (ii) The Car Chase (iii) Mammoth T.V. Studio

Performance length: 25 minutes

Composed: 1989   **Revised:**

Instruments: Flute, clarinet in B flat, trombone, violin I, violin II, cello, double bass, tuned percussion
Unpitched percussion: tambourine, suspended cymbals, clashed cymbals, bass drum, side drum with snares and gong (or tam-tam)

Publishing information: LONGMAN. Pack for sale containing teacher's book and parts book.

Recording details:

First performance: June 16 1989

at: Kirkwall Arts Theatre, Kirkwall, Orkney, for the St. Magnus Festival

by: Pupils of Kirkwall Grammar School, conducted by Glenys Hughes

Notes: Libretto by the composer. The general level of wind and string parts is approximately Grade IV/V Associated Board.

HIRCUS QUANDO BIBIT   (1989)

Catalogue no.:   J223

Descriptive title: HIRCUS QUANDO BIBIT

Musical format: Voice and piano

Location of manuscript: Mr Robin Yapp

Analysis:

Performance length: 1 minute

Composed: 1989   **Revised:**

Instruments: Mezzo-soprano and piano

Publishing information: MS

Recording details:

First performance: 20 June 1989

       at: The Old Brewery, Mere, Wiltshire

       by: Linda Hirst, mezzo-soprano and John Lenehan, piano

Notes: This was one of a number of short works which appeared on a wine list, the others being by Sir Harrison Birtwistle, Colin Matthews, Dominic Muldowney and John Woolrich. A tape recording is available at the National Sound Archive for private study only.

SYMPHONY NO. 4 (1989)

Catalogue no.: J224

Descriptive title: SYMPHONY NO. 4

Musical format: Full orchestra

Location of manuscript: Mrs Judy Arnold

Analysis: (i) *Moderato* (ii) *Allegro* (iii) *Adagio* (iv) *Andante - allegro* (without a break)

Performance length: 45 minutes

Composed: 1989 **Revised:**

Instruments: Two flutes (second doubling piccolo and alto flute), two oboes (second doubling cor anglais), two clarinets in A (second doubling bass clarinet in B flat), two bassoons (second doubling contrabassoon), two horns in F, two trumpets in C, timpani, strings

Publishing information: BOOSEY AND HAWKES. Pocket score for sale; full score and parts for hire.

Recording details:

First performance: September 10 1989

at: BBC Promenade Concert at the Royal Albert Hall, London

by: The Scottish Chamber Orchestra, conducted by the composer

Notes: Commissioned by Christian Salvesen plc for the Scottish Chamber Orchestra. A tape recording is available at the National Sound Archive for private study only.

HALLELUJAH! THE LORD GOD ALMICHTIE

(1989)

Catalogue no.:   J225

Descriptive title: HALLELUJAH! THE LORD GOD
ALMICHTIE for SATB chorus and organ

Musical format: Chorus and organ

Location of manuscript:

Analysis:

Performance length: 5 minutes

Composed: 1989   **Revised:**

Instruments: Soprano and Alto soli or small Soprano and Alto chorus,
Soprano, Alto, Tenor and Bass chorus and organ

Publishing information: CHESTER MUSIC. Full score for sale.

Recording details:

First performance: June 11 1989

          at: St. Giles' Church, Edinburgh

          by: The Choir of St. Paul's Church, conducted by Leslie
Shankland

Notes: Commissioned by St. Paul's Church, Edinburgh. The
text is early Scottish.

JUPITER LANDING   (1989)

Catalogue no.:   J226

Descriptive title: JUPITER LANDING. Music theatre work for children to play and sing.

Musical format: Children's opera

Location of manuscript: Mrs Judy Arnold

Analysis: One act

Performance length: 20 minutes

Composed: 1989   **Revised:**

Instruments: Children's solo voices, children's chorus, descant recorders or other melody instruments, pitched percussion (three parts ad lib.), unpitched percussion (three parts ad lib.)

Publishing information: LONGMAN. Sales pack containing teacher's book and parts book for sale (Spring 1991).

Recording details:

First performance: April 3 1990

    at: Queen Elizabeth Hall, London, as part of the Chldren's Day of the Maxwell Davies Festival at the South Bank Centre

    by: Pupils of the Close Side Primary School, Enfield, conducted by Mark Caswell

Notes: Libretto by the composer.

STRATHCLYDE CONCERTO NO. 3 (1989)

Catalogue no.:   J227

Descriptive title: STRATHCLYDE CONCERTO NO. 3 for
                                    horn, trumpet and orchestra

Musical format: Horn, trumpet and orchestra

Location of manuscript: Mrs Judy Arnold

Analysis: One continuous movement

Performance length: 30 minutes

Composed: 1989   **Revised:**

Instruments: Horn and trumpet solos, two flutes (second doubling alto
                     flute), two oboes (second doubling cor anglais), two
                     clarinets (second doubling bass clarinet), two bassoons
                     (second doubling contrabassoon), timpani, strings

Publishing information: BOOSEY AND HAWKES. Pocket score
                                    and horn and trumpet parts with piano
                                    reduction for sale; full score and parts
                                    for hire.

Recording details:

First performance: January 19 1990

    at: City Hall, Glasgow

    by: Robert Cook, horn and Peter Franks, trumpet and the
                     Scottish Chamber Orchestra, conducted by the
                     composer

Notes: Commissioned jointly by Strathclyde Regional
                     Council and the Scottish Chamber Orchestra with
                     funds provided by the Scottish Arts Council and
                     Strathclyde Regional Council. A tape recording is
                     available at the National Sound Archive for private
                     study only.

DINOSAUR AT LARGE   (1989)

Catalogue no.:   J228

Descriptive title: DINOSAUR AT LARGE. Music theatre work for children to play and sing.

Musical format: Children's opera

Location of manuscript: Mrs Judy Arnold

Analysis: One act

Performance length: 20 minutes

Composed: 1989   **Revised:**

Instruments: Children's solo voices, children's chorus, bugle, trumpet or cornet, melody instruments, pitched percussion
Unpitched percussion (4 players): *I* - suspended cymbal and gong (or tam-tam)
II - bass drum and small wood block
III - side drum and large woodblock
IV - tambourine

Publishing information: LONGMAN. Pack containing teacher's book and parts book on sale (Spring 1991).

Recording details:

First performance: July 4 1990

    at: Leeds Grammar School for the Leeds Festival

    by: Pupils of Pudsey Bolton Royds Junior School, conducted by Rose Hudson

Notes: Libretto by the composer.

THRENODY ON A PLAIN SONG
FOR MICHAEL VYNER   (1989)

Catalogue no.:   J229

Descriptive title:	THRENODY ON A PLAIN SONG FOR MICHAEL VYNER: Cor meum et caro mea exultaverunt in Deum
Musical format:	Full orchestra
Location of manuscript:	Mrs Judy Arnold, with a copy at the Glyndebourne Festival Opera Library

Analysis:

Performance length: 7 minutes

Composed: 1989   **Revised:**

Instruments: ?

Publishing information: CHESTER MUSIC.

Recording details:

First performance: October 25 1989

  at: Glyndebourne Opera House

  by: The London Sinfonietta, conducted by the composer

Notes:

ISLAND OF THE SAINTS   (?1990)

Catalogue no.:   J230

Descriptive title: ISLAND   OF   THE   SAINTS: INCIDENTAL MUSIC

Musical format:

Location of manuscript: Glenys Hughes

Analysis:

Performance length:

Composed: ?1990   **Revised:**

Instruments:

Publishing information:

Recording details:

First performance:

         at:

         by:

Notes: Written for the St. Magnus Festival, this piece comprises incidental music to a play by George Mackay Brown.

TRACTUS CLAUSUM ET RECONDITUM (1990)

Descriptive title: TRACTUS   CLAUSUM   ET RECONDITUM

Musical format: Voice and guitar

Location of manuscript: Mrs Judy Arnold

Analysis: One continuous movement

Performance length: 4 minutes

Composed: 1990   **Revised:**

Instruments: Mezzo-soprano, guitar

Publishing information: CHESTER MUSIC. Score for sale (in preparation).

Recording details:

First performance: May 20 1990

    at: Purcell Room, London

    by: Mary Thomas, mezzo-soprano and Timothy Walker, guitar

Notes:

DANGEROUS ERRAND (1990)

Catalogue no.: J232

Descriptive title: DANGEROUS ERRAND. Music theatre work for very young children to play and sing.

Musical format: Melody instruments, percussion and piano

Location of manuscript: Mrs Judy Arnold

Analysis: One act

Performance length: 15 minutes

Composed: 1990 **Revised:**

Instruments: Children's solo voices, children's chorus, melody instruments (recorders or substitutes), tuned percussion (four parts ad lib.)

Unpitched percussion (4 players): tambourine, side drum, suspended cymbal, bass drum, extra instruments ad lib.

Optional, simple accompaniment for piano (or keyboard or guitar)

Publishing information: LONGMAN. Pack containing teacher's book and parts book for sale (Spring 1991).

Recording details:

First performance: June 25 1990

at: Papdale Primary School, Kirkwall, Orkney, for the St. Magnus Festival

by: Pupils of Papdale Primary School, conducted by Glenys Hughes

Notes: Libretto by the composer.

STRATHCLYDE CONCERTO NO. 4 (1990)

Catalogue no.:   **J233**

Descriptive title: STRATHCLYDE CONCERTO NO. 4 for clarinet and orchestra

Musical format: Clarinet and orchestra

Location of manuscript: Mrs Judy Arnold

Analysis: One continuous movement: *Lento - allegro moderato - adagio - cadenza - andante*

Performance length: 20 minutes

Composed: 1990   **Revised:**

Instruments: Clarinet solo, two flutes (second doubling piccolo), two oboes, bass clarinet, two bassoons (second doubling contrabassoon), two horns, strings
Percussion (1 player): timpani, marimba, crotales, large Japanese temple gong

Publishing information: CHESTER MUSIC (in preparation).

Recording details:

First performance: November 21 1990

    at: City Hall, Glasgow

    by: Lewis Morrison, clarinet and the Scottish Chamber Orchestra, conducted by the composer.

Notes: Based on a 17th century tune by the blind folk musician Rory Dall Morrison.

CAROLINE MATHILDE (1990)

Catalogue no.: J234

Descriptive title: CAROLINE MATHILDE. Ballet in two acts

Musical format: Ballet

Location of manuscript: Mrs Judy Arnold

Analysis: Two acts

Performance length: 2 hours

Composed: 1990   **Revised:**

Instruments:

Publishing information:

Recording details:

First performance: (scheduled) March 14 1991

     at: Royal Theatre, Copenhagen

     by: Conductor, Markus Lehtinen

Notes: Commissioned by the Royal Danish Ballet. Choreography by Flemming Flindt. Originally planned to be entitled *Pandora's Box*.

HIGHBURY FLING   (1990)

Catalogue no.:   J235

Descriptive title: HIGHBURY FLING for piano

Musical format: Piano solo

Location of manuscript: Sheila McCrindle

Analysis:

Performance length:

Composed: 1990   **Revised:**

Instruments: Piano

Publishing information: MS

Recording details:

First performance:

      at:

      by:

Notes: For Sheila McCrindle.

CONCERTO No. 27   (1990)

Catalogue no.:   J236

Descriptive title: CONCERTO No. 27 for Partypopper
                                 and orchestra, arranged for piano

Musical format: Piano solo

Location of manuscript: The composer

Analysis:

Performance length:

Composed: 1990   **Revised:**

Instruments: Piano

Publishing information: MS

Recording details:

First performance:

       at:

       by:

Notes: For Tina Morrison.

LITTLE CHRISTMAS MUSIC   (1990)

Catalogue no.:   J237

Descriptive title: A LITTLE CHRISTMAS MUSIC

Musical format: Oboe and violin

Location of manuscript: The composer

Analysis:

Performance length:

Composed: 1990   **Revised:**

Instruments: Oboe, violin

Publishing information: MS

Recording details:

First performance:

       at:

       by:

Notes: For Ian Kellam.

APPLE BASKET: APPLE BLOSSOM (1990)

Catalogue no.: J238

Descriptive title: APPLE BASKET: APPLE BLOSSOM

Musical format: Unaccompanied chorus

Location of manuscript: Mrs Judy Arnold

Analysis: One continuous movement: *Andante flessibile - vivace - adagio*

Performance length:

Composed: 1990   **Revised:**

Instruments: Soprano, Alto, Tenor and Bass chorus (with piano part for rehearsal only)

Publishing information: CHESTER MUSIC. Full score for sale.

Recording details:

First performance: December 21 1990

    at: St. Alban's Church, Highgate, Birmingham

    by: The BBC Singers, conducted by Simon Jolly

Notes: Commissioned by the BBC Singers. Text by George Mackay Brown, from *Voyages*. Broadcast December 23 1990 on BBC Radio 3.

HYMN TO THE WORD OF GOD   (1990)

Catalogue no.:   J239

Descriptive title: HYMN TO THE WORD OF GOD: Motet

Musical format: Two tenor soli and SATB chorus with optional organ

Location of manuscript: Mrs Judy Arnold

Analysis:

Performance length: 4 minutes

Composed: 1990   **Revised:**

Instruments: Two Tenor soli, Soprano, Alto, Tenor and Bass chorus, optional organ

Publishing information: CHESTER MUSIC. Score (in preparation) for sale.

Recording details:

First performance: (scheduled) February 1991

    at: King's College, Cambridge

    by: The Choir of King's College, Cambridge, conducted by Stephen Cleobury

Notes: Commissioned by the Choir of King's College, Cambridge for its 500th anniversary. The text is Byzantine.

ALPHABETICAL LIST OF WORKS

BBC TALKS WITH OR ABOUT THE COMPOSER

'Composer's Portrait'
Talks about his music; includes a performance of the *String Quartet* by the English String Quartet.
November 22 1965

'Composers Today'
In discussion with Hans Werner Henze and Alexander Goehr about originality, 'newness' and tradition.
June 25 1967

'The Lively Arts'
Interviewed about *Missa Super L'Homme Armé* and *Revelation and Fall*.
February 28 1968

'Messiaen and the Music of Our Time'
Discussion with Alexander Goehr and Charles Groves.
March 12 1968

'Meet the Composer'
Introduces music of his own choice.
July 21 1969

'*Revelation and Fall*'
Stephen Walsh discusses the work.

'The Making of an Opera'
A discussion of *Taverner* with people involved with the first production.
July 15 1972

'The Conductor and the Composer'
    In conversation with Sir Charles Groves.
        March 16 1977

'The St. Magnus Festival'
    Talks about the Orkney Festival.
        June 24 1977

'Talking About Music no. 215'
    In conversation with Michael Berkeley.
        1977

'George Mackay Brown'
    George Mackay Brown introduces the first performance of
    Solstice of Light.
        October 2 1979

'Profile'
    A portrait of the composer.
        June 20 1980

'Kaleidoscope'
    Talks about *The Lighthouse*
        September 3 1980

'Festival Comment'
    Talks about *The Lighthouse* and the Fires of London concert at
    the 1980 Edinburgh International Festival.
        September 5 1980

'Music Weekly'
    Talks about the *Symphony no. 2*.
        March 8 1981

'Desert Island Discs'
> July 1 1983

'Kaleidoscope'
Talks about composing, and the importance of teaching music to children.
> September 4 1987

Interview
Talks about the success of the first twelve years of the St. Magnus Festival.
> August 22 1988

Interview
Talks about recent concertos and work with the Scottish Chamber Orchestra.
> September 30 1988

Interview
Talks to Michael Berkeley about his life and work, with particular reference to the *Symphony no. 4*.
> October 6 1989

'Listening To - Peter Maxwell Davies'
Michael Hall talks about the mediaeval influences of the *String Quartet* (1961). Performance by the Alberni String Quartet.

Recordings of all these talks are available for private study at the National Sound Archive.

U.K. ADDRESSES OF PUBLISHERS

Boosey and Hawkes Music Publishers
> The Hyde, Edgware Road, London NW9 6JN
> Tel.: (071) 205 3861 Fax: (071) 200 3737
> Telex: 89 25 811 Hawkes G

Chester Music Sales Ltd.
> Newmarket Road, Bury St. Edmunds, Suffolk IP33 3YB
> Tel.: (0284) 702600 Fax: (0284) 703401

Oxford University Press
> Walton Street, Oxford OX2 6DP
> Tel.: (0865) 56767 Telex: 837330

Schott and Co. Ltd.
> Brunswick Road, Ashford, Kent TN23 1DX
> Tel.: (0233) 628987 Fax: (0233) 610232

Longman Group U.K.
> Longman House, Burnt Mill, Harlow, Essex CM20 2JE
> Tel.: (0279) 26721 Fax: (0279) 31059 Group 3 & 2
> Telex: 81259 Longmm G

Novello and Co. Ltd.
> Fairfield Road, Borough Green, Sevenoaks, Kent TN15 8DT
> Tel.: (0732) 883261 Fax: (0732) 882978 Telex: 95583

Sir Peter Maxwell Davies with Lucy Rendall for whom he wrote 'Lullabye for Lucy'.

Judy Arnold

Sir Peter Maxwell Davies at his home at Hoy, Orkney Islands.

Ros Drinkwater — The Sunday Times

Sir Peter Maxwell Davies at his home at Hoy, Orkney Islands.

Ros Drinkwater — The Sunday Times